UNCLE BEN

UNCLE BEN

DAVID BRITTON

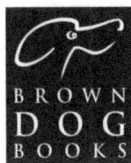

BROWN
DOG
BOOKS

First published 2018

Published under licence by Brown Dog Books and The Self-Publishing Partnership, 7 Green Park Station, Bath BA1 1JB

www.selfpublishingpartnership.co.uk

ISBN printed book: 978-1-78545-253-6
ISBN e-book: 978-1-178545-254-3

Printed and bound by CPI Group (UK) Ltd, Croydon, CR0 4YY

Cover design by Kevin Rylands

PREFACE

I first encountered Uncle Ben in 1947, after the unexpected death of my father. My mother decided to move us to her childhood home, the School House in Edmondsley, County Durham. In the attic, amongst the detritus of her parents' life, was a wooden trunk inscribed 'Sergeant B C Clayton 16th Durham Light Infantry'. Stapled to it was a brown paper label brittle with age, inscribed 'North Eastern Railway – Return to Chester Le Street station'.

Ben's trunk

Opening the lid revealed Treasure Trove. There was a 30-centimetre-long French bayonet with a wooden handle and a locking device to attach it to a rifle. Across the hilt was engraved 'St Etienne', presumably its place of manufacture. Alongside was a Pickelhaube made for a soldier with a small head. On the helmet was a brass double-headed eagle inscribed 'Gott Mit Uns'. In a drawer in the trunk was a bronze cap badge depicting a galloping horse; below its flying hooves were inscribed the words 'West Yorkshire'.

The chest had belonged to my mother's eldest brother, Ben Clayton, who went to France in 1915 with Kitchener's Army and had been killed near Ypres in 1917 as a Captain in the 2nd Battalion of the West Yorkshire Regiment. He had led an attack on a fortified farm known to the British Army as the 'Zonnebeke Redoubt' and died somewhere near it. For his bravery in capturing and holding the redoubt for several hours that day he was awarded the Military Cross. In civilian life he was an art teacher; during his 18 months at the front he sent home several sketchbooks of life in the trenches. These were in the bookcase in the living room. Some are serious, some descriptive and some are amusing.

After the war the workmen and deputies (foremen) of Edmondsley Colliery clubbed together to buy a gold fob watch that was presented, suitably inscribed, to my grandfather. Ben's younger brother, Tom, inherited the watch. Tom was conscripted at the age of 18, and had also served in France, as a sergeant in the Royal Field Artillery. I knew Uncle Tom well, but he never mentioned Uncle Ben or the First World War in my presence over the many years of our friendship, although I noted that he wore his father's gold fob watch almost every day. As he had no children, he left me the watch and his brother's Military Cross in his Will.

I decided to research Uncle Ben's time in the Army as best I could, before Armistice Day 2018 causes World War I to fade from our collective memory. I discovered that after eight months with a training battalion, the 16th Durham Light Infantry (DLI) in Darlington and on Cannock Chase, Ben had spent eight months in France as a sergeant in the 12th DLI before he was commissioned.

The campaigns of the 2nd Battalion of the West Yorkshire Regiment in 1916/17 had been published as a book in 1964. The book was based upon a field diary kept by the Commanding Officer of the 2nd West Yorks, Lieutenant Colonel James Jack. Ben Clayton appears several times in 'General Jack's Diary'.

Ben dated most of his sketches from the trenches, so they can be coordinated with the events described in General Jack's Diary. The Official War Diaries of 2nd West Yorks and of 12th Durham Light Infantry are available online and were also consulted.

CHAPTER ONE
ORIGINS

On the 16th of April 1890, Mary Chipchase married John Clayton in Easington, a mining town in County Durham. Mary was 21 years old, the daughter of a mining engineer, and probably saw herself as a member of the professional middle class. Her 26-year-old spouse describes himself in the Marriage Register that day as 'gentleman', but this was an aspiration rather than a reality. His father, Thomas Clayton, was a colliery heap keeper, a post for a responsible retired underground worker; his elder brother was a colliery joiner, and his two sisters were married to miners. When not at work, Thomas Clayton had developed skills akin to a physiotherapist and ran a successful business for miners with muscular strain injuries and back problems. The extra income allowed him to pursue his main interest as a Wesleyan Methodist local preacher and funded a university education for his younger son, John.

Thomas Clayton

John had walked into Durham University from nearby Pittington each day for two years to study for a Bachelor of Arts degree, paid for by his father. He graduated B.A. in the year of his marriage. Perhaps his aspiration to be seen as a gentleman was not misplaced, as he became a Justice of the Peace on Chester le Street Bench, a District Councillor for Edmondsley on Chester le Street Rural District Council, and had a model village named after him, Claytonville.

At the time of his wedding John was the assistant schoolmaster at the village primary school in Edmondsley, nine miles north west of Pittington.

Edmondsley Bank, 1913. The School and School House are
at the bottom of the hill on the right. The unfenced railway tracks are
just visible as they cross the road junction.

Married life for Mary started in rented accommodation on Daisy Hill, just over the 'bank top' from Edmondsley.

Daisy Hill sounds an ideal spot to begin married life, but the hamlet was at the centre of the Durham mining industry; six collieries, a brick works and two coke ovens were visible from the hilltop. A half-mile walk down the hill into Edmondsley brought John to his school, a 'British School' run by the non-conformist 'British and Foreign Bible Society'. About 300 pupils attended daily.

Edmondsley is a place name from Old English and probably translates as 'a shepherd's clearing', an apt enough description of the tillable plateau between the gorse and heather of Walridge Fell to the east and Charlaw Fell to the west. Wellington Pit had been sunk on the plateau in 1840 and two more collieries soon opened close by. In 1834 the Tyne and Stanhope railway had been built two miles away, the better to connect the Pennine lead mines of West Durham to the coast. A rail link to the Tyne from the collieries around Daisy Hill was the factor that would secure their long-term profitability. The gradient from the hilltop to the Tyne and Stanhope line was too steep for locomotives, so a giant stationary steam engine – the Sacriston Standing Engine – was constructed on the summit. Forty feet high, the wheelhouse straddled the colliery railway tracks that ran beneath it.

Sacriston Standing Engine on Daisy Hill, 1913

Laden coal wagons were pulled up to the Engine by steel hawsers controlled from the wheelhouse and then dispatched down the incline to Stella Gill in the steep valley of the Congburn where the locomotives of the Tyne and Stanhope Railway transported them to South Shields. The coal was cascaded into the holds of steam colliers and shipped worldwide out of the Tyne. The velocity of the laden wagons downhill pulled the returning empty trucks uphill along the single-track wagon way. Accurately positioned passing points with twin tracks prevented disaster.

John Clayton's walks to school crossed the unfenced railway from Wellington Pit, the hawser on cylindrical runners between the rails. A lengthy wait could ensue while laden wagons groaned up to the Standing Engine, the steel rope three or four feet off the ground humming with the strain.

This ingenious system ensured that Edmondsley was thriving

in 1890. The village had a Post Office connected to the National Telegraph, two small shops and two public houses. The main shop for the area was on Daisy Hill, just opposite the Standing Engine where Chester le Street Cooperative and Industrial Society had built an Art Nouveau double-fronted store. Sacks of rice, tapioca, semolina, tropical nuts, dried fruit and spices lay open on the floor, a source of unfamiliar fragrances. Female shop assistants used four-ounce and eight-ounce copper scoops to ladle the exotic fruits of Empire into brown paper bags. Cooperative Society profits were healthy and were distributed bi-annually to members according to past purchases.

Class divided Edmondsley. Dr Hall the local general practitioner, Mr Hodgson the mine manager, his deputy, the school headmaster Mr Johnson and his deputy John Clayton formed a tiny group of educated men, five in a population of two thousand. They were Wesleyan Methodists who attended chapel twice on Sunday, and sent their children to Sunday school. Social life for these families revolved around chapel functions, weekday coffee evenings, Bible classes, missionary groups and, in the summer, nature rambles. Alcohol and gambling were anathema.

In 1894, an annual figure of 150,000 tons of coal was extracted from Wellington Pit; 300 miners worked underground, extracting about 500 tons each from the coalface. They lived dangerous lives. In the winter a man could be underground before dawn, work in the darkness of the deep coal seams for eight hours or more, illuminated only by the flame of a Stephenson Safety Lamp (a 'Geordie Lamp'), and surface after dusk.

Since 1860, eighteen men had died underground in Edmondsley Colliery. Rock falls, flooding, firedamp explosions, accidents from moving coal tubs, shot firing and falls down the open shaft were regular occurrences. More than 50 miners had been seriously injured in that time and had been unable to work thereafter. Hewing coal in a gallery three feet high produced a regular toll of groin ruptures, head injuries, and slipped discs.

If a man could not work, he received no pay. Tommy Ramsay had argued that the same wage should be paid for each day's work throughout the Durham coalfield. Ramsay was from Pelton Fell, near Stella Gill, a Methodist Local Preacher, and an early leader of the district miners' union. On three occasions he attempted to persuade the Durham miners to emulate the Northumberland miners in forming a county combination. In 1873, a combination eventually took shape; Tommy Ramsay's portrait was the centrepiece of the Edmondsley Colliery Miners' Banner and was paraded each year through the streets of Durham by the miners and their families at the annual Miners' Gala, tunefully accompanied by Wellington Colliery Brass Band.

Edmondsley Colliery banner with Tommy Ramsay

A minority of miners sought relief from their harsh existence by indulgence in alcohol and gambling, with social consequences for their wives and offspring, but the majority were family men who raced pigeons and whippets, cultivated allotments, competed in Leek Shows, played cricket and soccer, and followed the fortunes of the First Division football clubs in Newcastle and Sunderland. Fishing for beck trout was available in the Congburn, and poaching for the pot was usually ignored by the local farmers, the better to preserve relations with the village.

Away from work, a fashionable miner wore a dark suit from the Co-op, a spotless white, silk scarf knotted around the neck as a cravat, and a smart flat cap. This stylish outfit was paraded at family celebrations, at important football matches, and at chapel or village assemblies. Primary education ended at the age of eleven, but adult education was available in the library and lecture rooms of the Mechanics Institute in Sacriston, just on the other side of Daisy Hill. A few determined men would eventually pass the examinations of the North of England Institute of Mining and Mechanical Engineers and became Chartered Mining Engineers. After 1903, both men and women could take part in Workers Education Association programmes in Edmondsley Primitive Methodist Chapel.

CHAPTER TWO
FAMILY

After four barren years Mary Clayton suddenly gave birth to Daisy (Margaret Elizabeth) Clayton on Daisy Hill in 1894, and to Benjamin Chipchase Clayton in 1895. A second son, Thomas Chipchase Clayton was born in 1897 at the School House in Edmondsley, just after John had been promoted to Headmaster of Edmondsley School.

School House is described in Kelly's Directory of 1910 as a 'superior detached house'. It had an entrance hall, three reception rooms, a kitchen with a cooking range and an open fire complete with a hob for the kettle. Behind the kitchen was a washhouse with a built-in washtub over a second open fire. The yard contained a coalhouse and a flushing lavatory. Upstairs there were three bedrooms and a bathroom, all with fireplaces. The garden contained a stable and hay store for a pony. A carriage house for a jaunting car faced the road at the bottom of the garden. The garden gate led into the adjacent schoolyard.

School House with John Clayton and Patchy, 1916

After three years in this stylish dwelling, Mary Clayton became pregnant again, but as this pregnancy proceeded she became increasingly unwell, and in June 1899 she died, aged 30. The Cause of Death was recorded as Puerperal Pneumonia, an overwhelming chest infection with septic consolidation of the lungs. Before antibiotics were discovered, treatment could only be supportive.

Mary died in the front bedroom at School House with her husband at her side, leaving three children under six and John Clayton a widower, aged 34. Daisy was five, Ben was four, and Tom was a two-year-old toddler.

The early years of the Boer War were desolate for the occupants of School House. The children were grieving for their mother. Their father had to suppress his feelings to cope with his role as a single parent. Passage through the garden gate meant that his thoughts had to switch from his children to his job, the source of their income and of their home, for the tenancy of School House depended upon his position as Headmaster.

In the Census of 31st March 1901 the occupants of School House are recorded as John Clayton, his children, his father, his widowed elder brother, and two nieces aged 17 and 18. The teenage girls may have been resident in the house at the time to support their cousins. To a neutral observer the Census return indicates that John Clayton was a man in need of a second wife.

On 10th September 1902, three years after Mary's death, he married Isabella Armstrong, a 35-year-old spinster from Sacriston, at Chester le Street Wesleyan Methodist Church. By Edwardian standards Isabel (sic) was a mature bride, but her maturity was the key to her success as a beloved stepmother of Mary's three, and soon as mother of her own offspring of two girls and a boy. Daisy was in third year at her father's school, Ben was a year behind, and Tom would be in the first form.

The arrival of a new baby, Priscilla, the routine of their days at their father's school next door, and Isabel's domesticity steadied their lives. In a sepia snap shot of 1904 the three of them seem happy and contented.

Daisy, Ben and Tom Clayton when children

By then Daisy, Ben and Tom were old enough to roam Arcadia, the streams, lakes, fells and valleys surrounding Edmondsley. There was a crumbling stone bridge on an ancient drovers' road in the precipitous valley of the Congburn, with a swimming hole nearby. Water voles, otters, deer, badgers, foxes, hedgehogs and birds of every sort were in abundance. In winter, bespoke wooden sledges with wrought iron runners could be purchased from the colliery blacksmith for a shilling (ten pence); the sledge could be ordered in the morning and be in action on Edmondsley Bank's icy slope in the afternoon. Direct Current electricity became available from the colliery generator throughout the village and oil lamps were soon a memory.

A hint of trouble ahead, unrecognised in the Edmondsley of

1906, was the launch of HMS Dreadnought, a battleship so advanced that all the other battleships in the enormous Royal Navy became obsolescent overnight. The Imperial German Navy recognised an opportunity and began to build a rival fleet of dreadnoughts, the better to challenge the century-long hegemony of the British at sea. A naval arms race had begun.

In 1910, a second catastrophe fell on the family. Daisy had been five when her mother died and eight when her father remarried. Being the eldest girl in the growing family, she was the sensible sister and unpaid nanny to her brother Tom and to Isabel's three, Priscilla, Bill and Rita. This had helped her come to terms with the loss of her mother. She was central to life in her family and much loved by her father and her stepmother.

In the winter of 1910 Daisy unexpectedly developed colicky abdominal pain that did not settle. The pain shifted to the right side of her abdomen and was accompanied by a high temperature. Her condition deteriorated so rapidly that Dr Hall was called in the night from his home at Mount Pleasant, about half a mile away. He diagnosed appendicitis. Daisy was taken to the County Hospital in Durham City about five miles away, but despite treatment she died there two days later, aged 16 years. Ben was 15, Tom was 13, Priscilla was six, Bill was four, and Rita just two. Mary's two sons were devastated and the elder two of Isabel's children very upset. John and Isabel's staunch Methodist Faith was tested, but they came to terms with Daisy's death and comforted their children.

CHAPTER 3
BEN'S EDUCATION AND
THE ONSET OF WAR

As a boy, Ben Clayton enjoyed painting; a watercolour of Wellington Pit that he painted when he was aged 14 is still in existence. Contemporary photographs of the colliery confirm that the portrayal is accurate, if somewhat naïve.

Edmondsley Colliery, 1913

Ben's watercolour of Edmondsley Colliery

John Clayton recognised Ben's talent and encouraged his son to study for his School Leaving Certificate in Mathematics, English and French, the entrance examination to higher education for a boy from his background.

Ben passed his School Certificate within the year, walking three miles down to Chester le Street Secondary School each day and three miles back again. In 1912, funded by his father, he enrolled as a student teacher of art at the City of Leeds Teachers' Training College, newly built in Beckett Park, Headingley.

Leeds Teachers' Training College

Although a mixed college, it was not coeducational in the modern sense. 300 women and 180 men lived on site in separate hostels, five for women and three for men. Each sex was taught in separate classes. A photograph of Ben as a student in Leeds, aged 18 in 1913, reveals quite the floppy haired, artistic, cool young dude.

Ben Clayton at art school, 1913

Ben Clayton spent almost three years in Leeds and sat his last examination, a National Examination in Drawing, at Rhyl Examination Centre in North Wales on 11ᵗʰ December 1914, four months after Great Britain had declared war on Germany. He submitted a pencil drawing of his grandfather, Thomas Clayton, and a watercolour of Saltburn Beach for perusal by the examiners.

Thomas Clayton sketched by Ben for art examination, 1914

The principal cause of the British Declaration in August 1914 was the remorseless naval arms race with Germany. The British Government had hesitated to support France and Russia at the outset of the conflict but victory by the Imperial German Army with the Imperial German Navy undefeated might have heralded an invasion of the British Isles.

There was immense social pressure for young men to join up as war fever seized every social class in Great Britain. The Newcastle Evening Chronicle of 3ʳᵈ September 1914 reports that men were still queuing a month after the Declaration of War to enlist at Fenham Barracks, Newcastle upon Tyne, the depot of both the Northumberland Fusiliers (NF) and the Durham Light Infantry (DLI). 600 recruits had left the city by train the night before, and on the morning of publication another 500 were despatched from the Central Station to enthusiastic applause from the crowds of patriotic onlookers, themselves only rarely going to fight.

> *'You smug faced crowds with kindling eye*
> *Who cheer when soldier lads march by*
> *Sneak home and pray you'll never know*
> *The hell where youth and laughter go.'*

Siegfried Sassoon, 1917

Four thousand volunteers from Durham and Northumberland went to Bullswater Camp near Woking in Surrey. There they formed the 10th and 11th (general) service battalions of the Northumberland Fusiliers and the 12th and 13th service battalions of the Durham Light Infantry; 'general' service meant that the soldiers had volunteered for overseas service.

The four battalions were brigaded together as the 68th Brigade of the 23rd Division and in August 1915 the Division was sent to France under a Major General James Melville Babington. Babington, a moustachioed Victorian cavalry officer, belied his image. A shrewd Scot, he ensured that his men were appropriately trained, properly equipped, and well shod before their embarkation for France.

In the Great War, the British Army fought in battalions of at the most a thousand men, identified for recruiting purposes with a regiment from a specific geographical area, hence 12th DLI, 13th DLI, 10th NF, 11th NF. Each battalion was commanded by a Lieutenant Colonel, with a Major second in command and each battalion was divided into four companies of perhaps 250 men, usually led by a captain. There were four platoons of about 60 men in each company, led by a Lieutenant or Second Lieutenant. Platoons were divided into sections of ten to fifteen soldiers led by a corporal.

Four battalions (about 4,000 men) formed a Brigade under a Brigadier General. Three Brigades formed a Division; with Divisional artillery and Divisional machine guns this amounted to 18,000–20,000 men, commanded by a Major General. Two or three divisions formed a Corps commanded by a Lieutenant General, and two Corps formed an Army, led by a General. A Field Marshal was the Commander in Chief of several armies – an Army Group.

Before the Great War there were usually only two regular battalions in a named British Regiment, one on Imperial Garrison Duty overseas and the other at home in Great Britain or Ireland. Both battalions were professional soldiers. They were supported by a Regimental Depot in or near the home county, and by reserve (retired regular) and territorial (local volunteer) battalions of part-time troops from that county. Recruitment into Kitchener's Army increased the number of battalions in every regiment exponentially.

CHAPTER FOUR
KITCHENER'S ARMY

Having passed his final examinations, Ben returned home from Leeds in December 1914, a qualified art teacher. His college had been converted into a military hospital to deal with the casualties of the British Expeditionary Force at the Battles of Mons, Le Cateau and First Ypres, so he had to complete his studies living in lodgings out of college. The Art Room where he had spent much time before the War had already been converted into the operating theatre because of the excellence of the natural light from the glass roof.

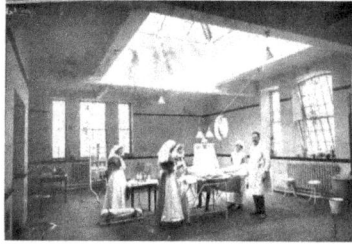

Art room operating theatre, 1914

Ben Clayton arrived back in Edmondsley on 15th December 1914. Next morning the Durham port of Hartlepool, some 30 miles away, was shelled at dawn by two German battle-cruisers, Seydlitz and Moltke, and by the heavy cruiser Blucher, all recent products of the naval arms race. The attack was completely unheralded and mayhem broke out as 1,150 shells hit the town in 45 minutes. One hundred and twelve civilians were killed, and 200 were wounded, many in both categories being children. The shelling was clearly audible to the Claytons at breakfast in School House before school.

A previous local incident had also brought the War closer to Edmondsley. A 'Zeppelin' (probably a Schütte-Lanz airship of the

Imperial Navy scouting for the Hartlepool Raid) had been seen a week or two earlier over Sunderland. A heap keeper, employed at Wellington Pit because he had lost a leg in the mine, went out onto the gantry between the loading bay and the spoil heap, the better to view the action. Jumping up and down with excitement, he entrapped his wooden leg between the planks. He had to disconnect it, crawl off the gantry, and hobble home with a makeshift crutch. His wife, daily help to Isabel Clayton, retrieved the leg from the colliery office later.

The front line in France had stabilised but manpower losses in the small regular British Army were critical and reinforcements from the Indian Army together with half-trained Territorial troops and older reservists were being rushed to the front. Ben attempted to enlist in Kitchener's Third Wave (K3) in January 1915 but the recruitment system was overwhelmed, so his particulars were taken and he was told to wait. After a term as a schoolteacher, he was called to attest in Sunderland as part of K4, perhaps presciently, on All Fools Day 1915.

He was 19 years and 11 months old, five feet nine and a half inches in height, and 12 stone in weight. He was much taller and heavier than the average English recruit of five foot seven and ten stone. The Approving Officer, a Major Squance, recognised his potential and promoted him to Corporal forthwith. This increased his daily pay from 13 pence to 21 pence, from about £5 in today's currency to £7.

Corporal Clayton, Number 24955, joined the 16th Durham Light Infantry in Darlington where he underwent basic training. After four months he was promoted to (unpaid) Lance Sergeant by his Commanding Officer.

Sergeant Ben Clayton, Durham Light Infantry, 1915

The 16th DLI was the principal local training organisation supplying drafts to the DLI battalions in France. In November 1915, the battalion was transferred by rail from Darlington to Rugeley Camp on Cannock Chase as training was becoming centralised.

TO MY BEST CHUM—MY FATHER.
Dear old Dad, when Kitchener called
  On me to come up with the Boys;
I thought of you and my dear old home,
  And the scenes of my childhood joys.
It's up to me to go out and help,
  The other brave chaps at the Front,
Never let it be said I was one that jibbed
  While others bore the brunt.
When "Ours" go where this picture tells
  And I hope that won't be long;
We'll get the Huns well on the run,
  To the tune of our marching song.

Postcard from Cannock Chase, 1915

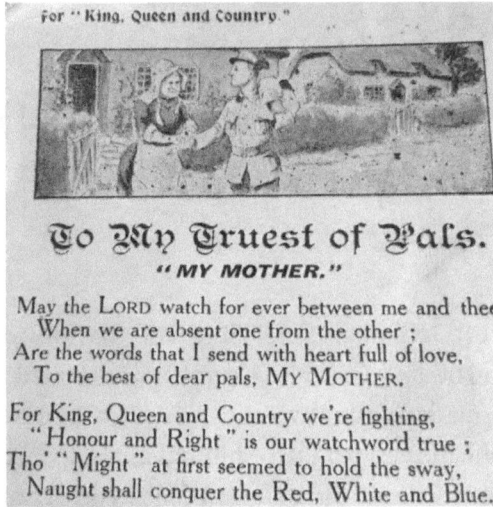

For " King, Queen and Country."

To My Truest of Pals.
" MY MOTHER."

May the LORD watch for ever between me and thee
    When we are absent one from the other ;
Are the words that I send with heart full of love,
    To the best of dear pals, MY MOTHER.

For King, Queen and Country we're fighting,
    " Honour and Right " is our watchword true ;
Tho' " Might " at first seemed to hold the sway,
    Naught shall conquer the Red, White and Blue.

Postcard from Cannock Chase, 1915

Rugeley could easily accommodate the 20,000 men of a division and was sending drafts daily to replace shattered formations at the front. A second camp, Brocton, was close by. Both camps consisted of bleak rows of draughty wooden Nissen Huts. Although both were supplied with electricity, water, medical services and a rail link, there was no Army Catering Corps on site. Food was cooked by the recruits on stoves in their huts and consumed on tables between the rows of beds. Over the next four years more than a million men were put through fitness training, basic drill, weapons training and field craft at Rugeley and Brocton in facsimiles of the British, French and German trench systems that were constructed on the Chase.

CHAPTER FIVE

FRANCE WITH THE DURHAM LIGHT INFANTRY

On the 17th of December 1915, Sergeant Clayton joined the 12th DLI near Armentières. On 20th December, his unpaid rank of Lance Sergeant was made substantive and thereafter, as a Sergeant rather than a Corporal, he was paid two shillings and sixpence a day, £13.25 in modern terms. The 68th Brigade had been in the Artois sector of the Western Front as part of the 23rd Division, IIIrd Corps, 4th Army for four months. It was manning trenches at the village of Bois-Grenier about a mile from Armentières.

Postcard of Allied flags from Armentières, 1915

The front around Armentières remained stable until 1918, and so was often used as a 'nursery sector' to accustom troops fresh from England to warfare in the trenches.

Trench life consisted of a 'Stand To' on the fire step at dawn and dusk, night time 'fatigues' (working parties) in no man's land to strengthen defences, and nocturnal trench raids to bomb the enemy with hand grenades or to capture prisoners. Sentry duty, sleep in dugouts excavated into the trench walls, delousing and writing letters to loved ones at home were daylight activities interrupted by avoidance of snipers and endemic enemy shelling. Cooking was mostly nocturnal, smoke being a target for enemy artillery.

The two DLI battalions relieved each other at night every five or six days, as did the two NF battalions. After relief, the troops spent another 48 hours in reserve trenches about half a mile behind the line to man fatigues for the Royal Engineers. They then proceeded into billets in barns and cottages four or five miles away. Farms were still being worked close to the front, albeit mostly by the elderly, but the steady rotation of weary battalions encouraged local entrepreneurs to provide estaminets and more unseemly services for the grateful soldiers.

Rats, dysentery and chest infections were constants. Lice in the creases of clothing may transmit life threatening Typhus. Artois had been fought over three times since 1914, so trench extension could lead to the opening of makeshift graves, the working parties then being faced with disintegrating corpses, maggots and the odours of liquefying intestines, sometimes of comrades or relatives who were recognisable.

The Germans had seized the high ground in 1914, so the December weather meant that the British trench systems were usually waterlogged. The wet trenches produced trench foot, which, with care, might have been avoided by the application of whale oil. Discovery of the condition could lead to a disciplinary charge and perhaps to Commanding Officer's Field Punishment when out of the line. This would consist of the guilty soldier being fettered to a post in a position of crucifixion for up to two hours, some three or four days at a time.

The water table (the Artesian Level) in the valley of the Lys was so close to the surface that British trenches inevitably filled with sewage. Shallow trenches were palisaded with sandbags or with decaying corpses to avoid sniping casualties. Artillery bombardment was endemic. 'Wizzbangs', high-velocity, 77-millimetre field gun projectiles with little time between the noise of arrival and the explosion, 'Jack Johnson's', higher-calibre howitzer shells named after the African-American Heavyweight Champion of the World because of their black smoke, and 'Minnies', low-velocity, 'Minenwerfer', heavy mortar shells, could all demolish the sodden palisades and arbitrarily produce death, or more nocturnal fatigues.

Sergeant Clayton joined 12th DLI behind the front at Erquinghem in time to see General Babington present Distinguished Conduct Medals to Corporal Hornby and Private Worton of 13th DLI. He had missed the ceremony two days earlier where General Pulteney, the Corps Commander, presented a miner from Wingate, a few miles from Durham, with the Victoria Cross. Private Thomas Kenny of 13th DLI had rescued Second Lieutenant Philip Brown who had been shot in both thighs while lost near the enemy parapet in a fog. Private Kenny carried Lieutenant Brown on his back into a shell hole from where he went to get help. He returned with a rescue party, but this was engaged by a sortie from the German trenches. Private Watt of West Hartlepool was killed. Second Lieutenant Brown was taken back to the British line, but died from his wounds. The two DLI soldiers were buried next to each other in the local cemetery. Lance Sergeant Kenny survived the war to die at his home in County Durham 33 years later, aged 66.

When Ben joined 12th DLI, 'other ranks' were strengthening defences around Erquinghem, while the officers languidly attended lectures about the use of gas. An enemy attack between Armentières and Ypres brought a smell of gas southwards on the wind, but the rain had stopped and the weather is described in the War Diary as mild and misty.

On 22nd December, Sergeant Clayton went into the trenches for the first time. The 12th DLI relieved the 9th Green Howards at La Rolanderie Farm just outside Erquinghem. La Rolanderie was (and is) a moated Flemish manor house with attached farm buildings on fenland just southeast of Armentières.

La Rolanderie Farm, 2017

The battalion was in the line for four very wet days, spending the winter solstice in muddy water four feet deep, being bombarded by the enemy artillery, a bombardment that continued throughout Christmas Day; the General Staff on both sides were determined there was to be no repeat of the Christmas Truces of 1914.

Ben must have contrasted his current circumstances with memories of Christmas Past, fires roaring in the rooms on both floors of School House, a Christmas tree in the hall, chestnuts roasting on the fires, dates and (non alcoholic) ginger wine in abundance, a Carol Service in Durham Cathedral on Christmas Eve, and the exchange of presents on Christmas morning, probably delivered on a working Christmas Eve by Daisy Hill Co-op.

The 12th DLI went back into billets on 26th December but Lieutenant Golden, the Machine Gun Officer, was killed whilst briefing the relieving officer. 12th DLI were out of the stinking flooded trenches until 30th December, when again they rotated with 13th DLI. The continual barrages had now levelled the trench parapets, so the battalion was instructed to rebuild and excavate throughout the darkness of New Year's Eve. On the night of 1st January 1916 the soldiers observed a failed trench raid by four officers and 78 men of the neighbouring 10th NF under Captain Norfolk. The Germans detected the Fusiliers in no man's land, and after illuminating them with flares and searchlights, killed six and wounded 20, including Captain Norfolk. 12th DLI and 10th NF remained in the line until 3rd January.

The casualty list for the 68th Brigade recorded in the War Diary on New Year's Eve reveals that 48 men had been killed and 177 were incapacitated or missing since August 1915, so the casualties from Captain Norfolk's raid were unusual. On 7th January the 68th Brigade marched into rest billets, the four battalions being widely dispersed. 12th DLI went to Fort Rompu, a hamlet in the Lys valley, a border strongpoint in past wars. Because it was the site of a massive brewery, when war was declared the village was evacuated, and the huge buildings were requisitioned by the British Army as a base and a hospital.

Fort Rompu brewery, 1916

On 15th January, 68th Brigade returned to the line at Rue Marle, and it was there that Sergeant Clayton began his Sketches from the

Trenches. The first sketch, dated 18/1/16, was undertaken on a dull misty day as British six-inch howitzers obliterated a fortified German machine gun emplacement nearby, blowing away the top, both sides and the Spandau gunners simultaneously.

The sketch depicts a Sergeant Fisher reclining on a futon of sandbags in a dugout built into the wall of a trench.

Sergeant Fisher in his dugout.

The dugout contains a separate storage area, an earthenware keg of rum, a water bottle on a hook, and Fisher's rifle propped against the wall. The rifle does not appear to be a standard snub-nosed Short Magazine Lee-Enfield, so perhaps Sergeant Fisher was a sniper and was equipped with a Pattern 1914 Enfield rifle – a P14. This rifle was a British adaptation of the Mauser rifles used by the Boers and was favoured as a sniper's rifle because it was more accurate than the Short Magazine Lee-Enfield.

Fisher is wearing a 1915 'Gor Blimey' cap, a 'Cap, Winter Service Dress' devised because balaclavas would not fit beneath standard 1915 forage caps. The 'Gor Blimey' was specifically allowed only on active service. It was not Standard Dress, as the internal wire stiffener had been removed. This caused controversy with unsympathetic senior officers. In 'Goodbye to All That' Robert Graves reports that the Colonel of his battalion, 2nd Royal Welch Fusiliers, forbade any deviation from standard clothing whatsoever, even in the depth of winter. Lieutenant Colonel Elwes, the Commanding Officer of the 12th DLI was an old soldier who had seen service in South Africa and India. He seems to have been more concerned with the welfare of his troops than with a strict rigidity of the dress code.

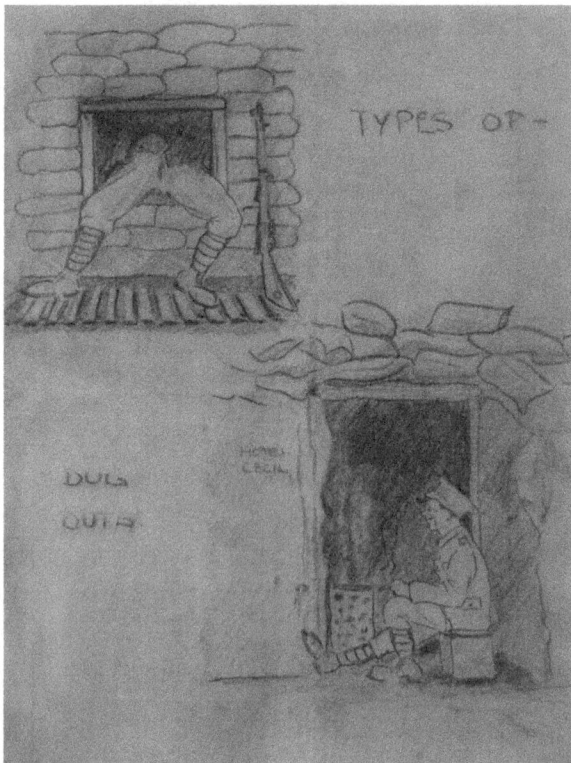

Types of dugouts

Between the 19th and the 23rd January, 12th DLI went into reserve. Soldiers billeted in Fort Rompu were allowed into Armentières where the civilian population still clung doggedly to pre-war life as enemy shelling wrecked their town. Sergeant Clayton must have been able to go into Armentières, as he sketched a relic from a shelled church in the town, a classical sculpture of the head of a young woman with her hair tied up in a hair band. This seems to be a depiction of St Joan of Arc, possibly from the Eglise Notre Dame du Sacré-Cœur in Rue Jeanne D'Arc in Armentières.

A relic from a shelled church of Armentières

Back in the trenches at Rue Marle again, on 26th January the enemy artillery obliterated the Signals dugout of 12th DLI killing five of the signalmen and wounding the other two. Taube aircraft could be seen circling around to direct fire. They were too high to be engaged from the ground, although just 12 years had passed since Orville Wright had made a very tentative First Flight in December 1903. The following day was Kaiser Wilhelm's birthday, and celebrated by incessant German artillery fire. A patrol under a 12th DLI officer into no man's land, led by Lieutenant Lafone, was sandwiched between two German patrols. Lieutenant Lafone's patrol was lucky to return to the line with only one man wounded.

Three days later, Sergeant Clayton sketched a sentry on the fire-step, an explanatory note alongside. A hazy full moon is obscured by cloud. The sentry's head seems needlessly exposed above the parapet ('para pete'- protect the head), although the height of the parados (the back wall of the trench 'para dos' – protect the back) is not apparent. The soldier is equipped with a Brodie steel helmet, unusual at the time as it was only patented in August 1915. He is wearing a sleeveless fur coat, gumboots and waders. His rifle is a standard snub-nosed Short Magazine Lee-Enfield and has an 18-inch bayonet fixed to it.

On the fire step

Ben comments that the helmet is an anti-shrapnel device, that waterproof footwear and waders are necessary because the trenches are regularly flooded to a level of four or five feet, and that fur coats are essential to keep out the cold of a January night.

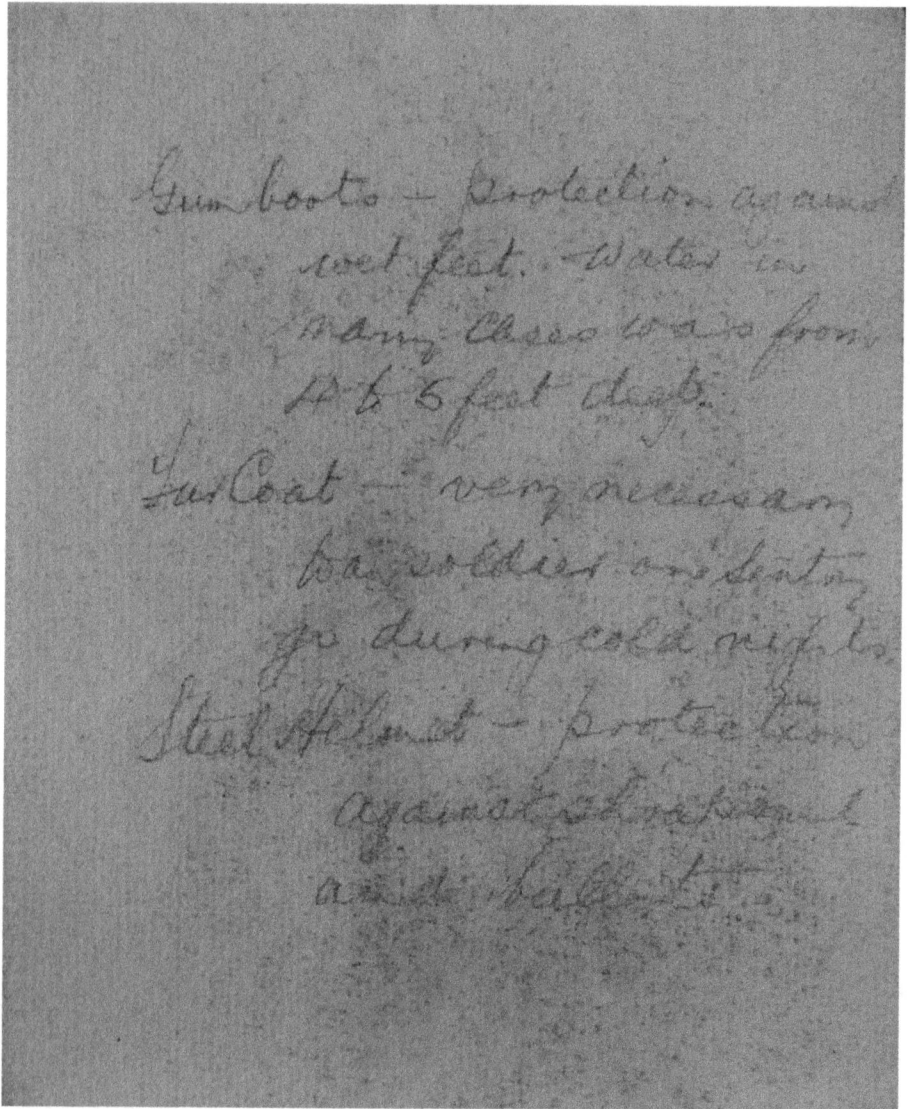

Fire step explanation

The battalion returned to divisional reserve next day, alternate halves being rostered nightly for working parties but on 17th February they again returned to the trench line at La Rolanderie.

CHAPTER SIX

'GERMINAL'

Next day, Brigadier General H Page Croft assumed command of the 68th Brigade. This wealthy Etonian Conservative MP had supported Ulster in 1913 when an Irish Civil War about Home Rule seemed imminent. A brave man and a patriot, Croft had gone to France in 1914, aged 33, with his territorial battalion. He was the first Territorial soldier to command a brigade but was also the first to be relieved of command because in 1916, still a sitting MP, he persisted in reporting the shortcomings of the British Army to his colleagues in the House of Commons. Loss of the 68th Brigade had little effect on his career. After many years in the Commons, Croft was ennobled during World War II and made Under-Secretary of State for War by Mr Churchill.

The day after Brigadier General Page Croft arrived, Ben sketched 'Tommy at Dinner' (lunch) again with a Gor Blimey trench cap, earmuffs raised, good boots, puttees and two tin-plate metal canteens. Tommy is sitting with his legs akimbo on a low shelf, eating his meal with a knife and fork rather than a spoon. He seems well shod, well fed, well supplied, dry and content, confirmation that at the time supply was not a problem in the sector and that the British Army was not very hard pressed, although two German aircraft bombed the area that day

Tommy at dinner

Thirty-six Cadets from Blendeques, St Omer, visited on 16th February. These were men selected for officer training from troops already in France. Their presence may have been a factor in persuading Sergeant Clayton to apply for a commission. At the time the uniform of officers in the British Army was easily distinguishable from that of other ranks, so casualties amongst subalterns were disproportionately high. Ranker replacements were accepted as inevitable by the decreasing number of surviving regular officers, but 'temporary officers' were often disparaged socially.

The 68th Brigade War Diary reports unrelenting frost and snow in mid February 1916, probably the cause of a quiet front with no more than desultory shelling and sniping. On 18th February, Sergeant Clayton had time to sketch a house that had been wrecked by shellfire but was still occupied, only 1,000 yards from the line;

A shelled house

On 20th February he produced a portrait of Old Bill, a middle aged soldier with two medal ribbons from the Boer War reflectively smoking a pipe.

Old Bill

In using the soubriquet 'Old Bill', Ben is acknowledging the immense popularity of the humorous and sardonic sketches produced during the previous winter in the 'Bystander' magazine by Lieutenant Bruce Bairnsfather, an officer with the Royal Warwickshire Regiment in France. To widespread acclaim, Bairnsfather published his first book, 'Fragments From France' in January 1915. The main character is a moustachioed private, 'Old Bill', 'first discovered in the alluvial deposits of Southern Flanders. Feeds almost exclusively on jam and water biscuits. Hobby: filling sandbags on dark and rainy nights!' Ben Clayton's Old Bill is a portrait of a real soldier rather than a cartoon, but Ben's soldier portrays the same attributes of phlegmatic experience and discipline as Bairnsfather's original.

On 26th February, the battalion marched 'without difficulty' according to the War Diary, 17 miles into billets in Morbecque. A week later it was joined by 13th DLI and the two battalions entrained for Marles-les-Mines, 16 miles south of Armentières. 12th DLI were billeted at Auchel where Sergeant Clayton probably experienced 'déjà vu.' Winding gear, spoil heaps and mining villages were all around him as described by Emil Zola in 'Germinal'. Daisy Hill reborn in Artois. Five months beforehand the British Army had sustained a costly defeat at Loos en Gohelle near Lens only six miles to the southeast.

The DLI and NF battalions were drawn up next day among the slag heaps and inspected by their new Corps Commander, Lieutenant General Henry Wilson of Fourth Corps. Lieutenant General Wilson's sangfroid allowed him to disregard a coincidental bombing raid by two German Aircraft that attacked the area whilst he was taking the salute.

A week of familiarisation followed before the Brigade entered trenches at Calonne near Marles les Mines. Most of the houses in both villages had been flattened by shellfire but the cellars were dry despite falling snow. These were converted into dugouts and equipped with salvaged furniture from the rooms above. The general opinion was that the Calonne lines were warmer, safer and more comfortable than the Armentières trenches, although noisome smells from the decomposing dead of the recent battle and the size of the local rats were both unsettling.

A poignant episode on 19th March was the death in action of the adjutant of 10th NF, Captain the Honourable S Joicey, son of Lord Joicey of Chester le Street, the one time MP for the Chester le Street Constituency that included Edmondsley. The Joicey mining company owned many mines around Edmondsley. During the night Captain Joicey was returning from a sap near the German line when an enemy hand grenade killed him. In the morning, his body was spotted in no man's land. An attempt to retrieve it produced a barrage of accurate small arms fire that allowed the enemy to seize the corpse. A fusillade from one of the 13th DLI's sections under a Lance Corporal Robinson then dispersed the German covering party of 30, killing and wounding several of them, although at a cost of two killed and two wounded in the 13th DLI.

Whilst stationed at Calonne, Sergeant Clayton sketched a 12th DLI Lance Corporal, one of his own section commanders, who is standing erect, wearing waders and smoking his pipe in a deep and stoutly constructed trench that towers at least 12 inches above him. His feet are on duckboards, implying that the heavy snowfalls had made the front-line fire trenches prone to flooding in contrast to the cellars in the ruined houses.

A Lance Corporal in the trenches at Calonne

When in reserve the 12th DLI was stationed at the Chateau d'Olhain, a chateau and estate at Fresnicourt le Dolmen, a farming village behind the line at Grenay and Bully Les Mines, six miles south of Auchel and Marles Les Mines. The castle, a moated, mediaeval fortress, had been requisitioned by the French Army at the outbreak of the War, and eventually handed over to the British.

Chateau d'Olhain stable yard, 2017

Here in April 1916, Sergeant Clayton sketched a study of 'Tommy out of the trenches', a picture of a reflective sergeant, well shod, a pipe in his mouth, seated with a strategically placed carafe and metal cup close at hand on a barrel.

A sergeant smoking a pipe

The next two sketches were also done at Fresnicourt. One is recognisable from contemporary photographs as a view of the stable yard at Chateau d'Olhain;

The stable yard, 1916

a groom in puttees is leaning nonchalantly on a stable door while a Coq Gaulois complete with erect tail plumage struts around the yard. The other is entitled 'C'est la Guerre', and shows an elderly couple in sabots (clogs), 19th-century French peasants still resignedly working the land because all the young men are away at the War.

'Les cultivateurs veterans'

They were probably tenants on the flat and fertile fields around Chateau d'Olhain.

April passed uneventfully in the line at Bully les Mines. On 18th April, a Captain Pease of 12th DLI led a raiding party that discovered that some new enemy saps had been abandoned and the next day 68th Brigade were relieved. They left the front line at Bully/Grenay for the last time and marched back into billets. Sergeant Clayton sketched one of the soldiers 'coming out for a rest'.

Coming out for a rest.

Into Reserve

The soldier is smoking a Woodbine and leaning slightly backwards. The weight of his 'Christmas Tree' of kit is obvious with rifle, steel helmet, laden rucksack, trenching tools and spare boots all slung on his back. His forage cap is pulled down over his brow and a look of relieved anticipation is visible on his face.

The 26th April 1916, the first day of the Easter Rising, was warm and spring like in Artois. Working parties of the 68th Brigade were strengthening local defences under the direction of the Royal Engineers; the War Diary makes no mention of the Irish Rebellion. The main military activity for 12th DLI that week was musketry and bombing practice in anticipation of a transfer further south to relieve the French Army of Artois around Souchez. As the British Army now had ten full divisions in France, British troops were being moved to the sector to allow the French to proceed to Verdun, where the grim battle of attrition had been raging for the past two months.

Vimy Ridge and the neighbouring ridge at Notre Dame de Lorrette dominate the area. The French had retaken Souchez and Lorrette at the time of Loos, but the Germans, 'gallant allies' of the Irish rebels, had repelled all assaults on Vimy. The British were disconcerted to find that the trenches at Lorrette and Souchez were unsafe, being too shallow and overlooked by the enemy on Vimy Ridge. Bodies from the French attacks were unburied or only superficially interred in the trench walls. Trench fortification was a priority but nightly enemy sniping and shelling intervened, illuminated by flares. Mining of Vimy Ridge was viewed as a strategy likely to gain the initiative but this had to be undertaken silently to avoid counter-mining. A hollow awl was screwed into the Artois chalk, and water poured in until the contents of the awl liquefied. The awl was then removed, the watery chalk collected, and the process repeated indefinitely. Passageways and large galleries could be constructed without much noise throughout the limestone strata.

During the naval battle off Jutland at the end of May 1916, the subterranean advances of the Durham and Northumberland miners unexpectedly produced a fierce reaction from the Germans. 70,000 shells, the heaviest bombardment ever experienced by the British Army, fell on the soldiers of the 47th (London) Division who were in trenches below Vimy Ridge, just to the right of the 23rd Division on Lorrette Ridge. A German Mine was detonated and the enemy infantry overran the 47th Division's front line.

On Sergeant Clayton's 21st Birthday, Lieutenant Colonel Elwes, the Officer Commanding 12th DLI, commissioned into the regiment ten years before Ben's birth and 'a dugout' in 1914, a retired officer recalled to the Colours, was unexpectedly evacuated from the battlefield with his second in command, Major Danvers, both officers apparently having 'cracked up' with shell shock under the horrendous bombardment. Command of 12th DLI fell on a Captain Arnott of the East Lancashire Regiment. Shell shock was a common experience of

front-line soldiers in all armies in the Great War, but in the British
Army the condition was only dealt with discreetly when senior officers
were afflicted. For other ranks, and occasionally for junior officers, a
Court Martial for Cowardice in the Face of the Enemy could result in
death at dawn at the hands of a firing squad.

Heavy shelling completely destroyed Souchez, the 68th Brigade
War Diary recording that the 12th DLI was having a 'warm time' in
the ruined town. On May 16th, Sergeant Clayton sketched the church
at Ablain St. Nazaire, the site of the 23rd Division's artillery, a mile or
so behind Souchez. The sketch reveals a facsimile of Fountains' Abbey
in France, a roofless gothic church wrecked by shellfire.

Ablain St Nazaire near Vimy Ridge

The shelled church at Ablain St Nazaire, August 2017

CHAPTER SEVEN

A COMMISSION

Ben Clayton had been identified as officer material on the day he joined the Army. After six months as a sergeant on the Western Front, he was posted to the GHQ Officer Cadet Training School at Blendeques near St Omer, a month after his 21st birthday. He was never to serve with the DLI again.

Sergeant Clayton went to Blendeques on 1st July, straight from the trenches. There was a convalescent camp nearby, 'No 4 Stationary Field Hospital', that dealt with patients suffering from dental, optical and skin problems. This tented hospital was in the grounds of a manor house at Arques, just across the River Blequin from Blendeques. On arrival from the trenches, Cadets assembled in the baths at the hospital, where they were deloused and had their uniforms steam-cleaned. Badges of rank were removed and replaced by armbands that displayed the initials of the Cadet School Infantry Company. The candidates spent the first part of their stay at Blendeques in the probationary sections of three cadet schools, Somerset, Beresford, and Marlborough. Probation consisted of a thorough revision of the Infantry Training received by other ranks, with an emphasis on the care of weapons, arms drill, lectures and nightly fatigues. Those who were judged suitable were then posted to one of the three schools and trained in Platoon and Company Infantry Tactics. Each day, half the Cadets filled the positions they would encounter as subalterns in the front line and the other half acted as critics, reviewing the actions of their peers in classroom debriefs. A short period in the trenches followed, attached to an unfamiliar platoon commander under enemy fire. The written reports of the instructors were final. Failure would result in the aspirant being returned to his unit.

If a candidate passed Infantry School, he was allowed to choose the regiment into which he wished to be commissioned, and could indent for an officer's uniform in that regiment, which he would pay for later by instalments. To avoid a conflict of interest, the new officer was usually not commissioned into a regiment in which he had served previously.

Following his commission as a Temporary Second Lieutenant, Ben Clayton was posted to the 2nd Battalion of The Prince of Wales's Own West Yorkshire Regiment, a regular battalion that had traditionally recruited from surroundings familiar to him in his student days, Leeds, Bradford and the West Riding of Yorkshire.

Second Lieutenant Benjamin Chipchase Clayton,
Prince of Wales's Own West Yorkshire Regiment, 1916

Cadet Clayton sketched the Stationary Hospital at Arques on 11th August, at the end of his time at Blendeques. By that time Ben had passed his course and had enjoyed a period of leave in Edmondsley where he purchased much of his subaltern's trench kit from the Co-op in Chester le Street and took a drill parade for the senior boys of Edmondsley School in the Upper Schoolyard. According to his father's, the Headmaster's, record of 'Edmondsley School during the War', the latter event was much enjoyed by all.

The Arques sketch is of the demesne of a manor house, with a river in the foreground. Between the house and the river there are seven bell tents and 14 military marquees set in an attractive landscape of trees, grassland and reeds along the bank of the river. There is no evidence of damage from bombardment. The portrayal is of a peaceful and attractive riverside, far from the War.

Arques hospital

Within eight months of arriving in France, casualties among infantry subalterns had elevated Ben Clayton, an art teacher from a Northern Methodist tradition into a band of brothers known for their bravery under fire, their wealth, their public-school education, their arrogance, and, not least, for their thoughtful paternalism towards the private soldier. That this was a big step for a man from Ben's background is confirmed by his next sketch 'Officers I have met'. This portrays two thin young men of his age in smart military attire with regulation pencil moustaches, both of whom affect a somewhat unreal air of languid entitlement.

Officers I have met

Perhaps the portrayal is a telling record of his own uncertainty as a country schoolmaster's son from County Durham about to enter a new world, although Ben seems to have adapted to the manners and traditions of the Officers' Mess without too much difficulty. A tinted photographic portrait of him in his Second Lieutenant's uniform, with a Sam Browne belt and a pencil moustache of his own, was to hang in the sitting room at School House for more than fifty years.

Militarily his position would not have been so different from the one he was leaving, as his sergeant's stripes would have accustomed him to command and to some privilege.

This and his education may have given him a degree of social confidence. His next sketch portrays three Second Lieutenants grouped around a piano in their billet singing 'You call me Baby Doll' and 'All that I ask is Love', accompanied by an accordion and a dog. Their bearded French landlord stands at the door waving his hands, and protesting 'Music Nappoo' (British Army slang for 'Ne Plus' – No More) 'M'sieur, Allez Coucher'.

A musical evening

Second Lieutenant Clayton joined the 2nd Battalion of the Prince of Wales's Own West Yorkshire Regiment on 14th August. The 2nd West Yorks was a battalion of regulars, brigaded at Southampton in September 1914 with three other regular battalions, the 2nd Scottish Rifles (Cameronians), 2nd Middlesex Regiment, and the 2nd Battalion of the Devonshire Regiment, thus forming the 23rd Brigade. The four battalions had been on garrison duty in the Mediterranean, the Devons being in Cairo and the other three in Malta. They all returned home relatively quickly and, together with the 24th and 25th Brigades of returning garrison troops, were mustered into the regular 8th Division at Winchester.

They sailed for Le Havre under Major General FJ Davies on 7th November 1914 and joined Fourth Corps under Lieutenant General Sir Henry Rawlinson (Bart). Rawlinson had inspected the division in Winchester before it embarked and recorded that garrison duty had softened the soldiers. Although excellent riflemen, they lacked trench mortars and had no training in the use of grenades. The divisional artillery was obsolescent and illness among the ranks was unusually high as the long absences abroad meant that they had little herd immunity from prevalent European infections. In spite of these problems the 2nd West Yorks were not at first found wanting in France; as experienced regulars under trusted officers they adapted rapidly to European warfare and to their lack of appropriate weaponry.

By the time Second Lieutenant Clayton joined them, most of the officers and other ranks who had returned so excitedly from Malta two years before were dead, killed by withering machine gunfire in doomed frontal advances at Neuve Chapelle, Aubers Ridge and on the First Day of the Somme. At zero hour on the Somme, 1st July 1916, 2nd West Yorks had advanced in open formation slightly downhill for 600 yards over poppy fields in full view of the enemy. The battalion was destroyed by elevated long-range Spandau fire from the hills opposite before it even reached the British wire. The enemy fire was so effective that the order for the 2nd Cameronians to follow the 2nd West Yorks was cancelled. The residue of the battalion that returned from Malta had ceased to exist. The 2nd West Yorks lost 16 officers and 490 other ranks out of a complement of 21 officers and 702 other ranks, leaving a residue of five officers and 212 other ranks, most of whom were already replacements for the loss in previous unsuccessful frontal attacks against the German Army.

The remnants of the 8th Division were sent back, not for much needed rest and recreation, but to the trenches behind the site of the British defeat at Loos. On 14th August, Second Lieutenant Clayton joined the despondent 2nd West Yorks near Beuvry in the dreary coalfields of the Loos Salient, all too familiar to him from his experiences with 12th DLI. He was accompanied by a draft of 200 Geordie Miners from Durham and Northumberland providing a further déjà vu, and by another newly commissioned officer from Blendeques, Second Lieutenant Matthew McConville. McConville was to establish a stellar reputation as a daredevil trench raider before volunteering for pilot training in the Royal Flying Corps about a year later where he was to suffer a serious wound in the face in a dogfight over the trenches.

CHAPTER EIGHT

A WEST YORKS SUBALTERN

Forty-eight hours before Second Lieutenant Clayton's arrival, the enemy raided the 2nd West Yorks trenches at night for a second time in as many weeks, further reducing morale and producing more casualties, although four Bavarian raiders were captured. A 23rd Brigade Court of Enquiry could not assign blame for these events other than to the fighting spirit of the enemy. Seven days later, Lieutenant Colonel L Hume-Spry, born in India and a Boer War Veteran, the Officer Commanding 2nd West Yorks, left the battalion to be replaced by Major James L Jack of the neighbouring 2nd Scottish Rifles (Cameronians). At the end of the month, Brigadier General E. Fagan of Jacob's Horse, Indian Army, replaced the 23rd Brigade commander, Brigadier General H D Tuson, who was mourning the loss of his only son at Jutland eight weeks before. Jutland, the first day of the Somme and the blood bath of the Loos Salient acted as a new broom for the senior ranks of the 2nd West Yorks.

Major Jack was an experienced regular officer, in 1914 a Captain in the Scottish Rifles who had served in the Boer War. He had spent the first two years of the Great War almost continuously at the front before being promoted to Lieutenant Colonel of the 2nd West Yorks a week or so after the arrival of Second Lieutenant Clayton and Second Lieutenant McConville. Captain Sidney Rogerson describes Jack in 'Twelve Days on the Somme, A Memoir of the Trenches, 1916' as 'punctilious, a disciplinarian, querulous if crossed, brave, energetic, and a real friend to his officers and therefore to his men'. Jack was determined to maintain the proprieties of pre-war life, and Rogerson quotes him 'There is no need to live like a pig, even though one is surrounded by filth.'

Major General R C Money, a fellow Cameronian who knew Jack

from pre-war days, describes him as intensely reserved with great
nervous energy; a man who had no close friends, he regularly drove
himself ultra vires. Lieutenant McConville later recorded 'he had
the knack of lifting the barrier of rank and striking a personal note
of man to man encouragement which, after his entirely unaffected
contempt for his own safety and comfort, was the secret of his place
in the spontaneous respect of every man in his command.'

Lieutenant Colonel Jack was clearly a stalwart Scottish Officer
of the Old School, much respected by his peers for his approach to
the welfare of the front-line infantry. He ended the Great War as a
Brigadier General and wrote a diary about his time in France with the
Scottish Rifles and 2nd West Yorks that was edited by John Terraine
and published in 1964, a few weeks after Jack's death.

Rogerson describes the area in the Loos Salient occupied by the
2nd West Yorks as 'a putrid bone yard' filled with superficially buried
corpses, and reeking of death. Men vomited when attempting to
dig new trenches as with every yard rotting bodies were unearthed.
The trench parapets were constructed with corpses thinly hidden by
rotting sandbags that were occupied by huge noisy rats replete with
human flesh' (Abridged).

Lieutenant Colonel Jack was to remain Second Lieutenant
Clayton's commanding officer for the next twelve months. From his
remarks about Ben in 'General Jack's Diary', the Colonel thought well
of his new subaltern, and was to approve Ben's promotion over the
following twelve months to the rank of Captain.

Colonel Jack's method of restoring the morale of the shaken
battalion was, according to McConville, based upon personal example,
regular routine and pre-war standards. From the day of his arrival, Jack
insisted on a life of discipline and regularity for 2nd West Yorks when
they were out of the line. A sick parade at 7 a.m. for soldiers unfit for
duty was followed by 15 minutes of physical exercise for all healthy
troops on the ration strength. An hour for breakfast was followed by
forty-five minutes of close-order drill under the Regimental Sergeant

Major. The whole battalion undertook this with the drums on parade, and officers of less than one year's service in the ranks. The battalion then undertook exercises in tactical training, musketry, and bayonet practice followed by a march past the Battalion Commander with the drums and fifes playing. After lunch ('dinner'), specialist classes for all ranks were held in bombing, scouting, signalling, machine gun management, cooking and transport under the appropriate experts. A second sick parade was held for trivial cases followed by a formal mounting of the guard under the Adjutant, this being attended by officers of less than one year's service, field punishment men, and defaulters. The fifes and drums then beat 'Retreat' before a period of free time, followed by supper and 'lights out'.

Ben joined C Company under a Captain Hawley, a regular who had seen years of service in West Africa. Several of the senior officers were by now from a colonial background as a result of the unceasing casualties. Major McLaren, the second in command, was from Ontario, Lieutenant Peter Palmes was a Rhodesian farmer in civilian life, Second Lieutenant Sankey, commanding D Company, and Second Lieutenant Matheson, the temporary Adjutant, were Canadians.

On 1st September, the battalion relieved the 2nd Battalion of the Rifle Brigade in the front trenches at Vermelles in the flat lands of Artois, just to the southwest of the most formidable fortress on the Western Front, the interlocking trenches and pillboxes of the Hohenzollern Redoubt. The Redoubt had been created to defend the large spoil heap (crassier) produced by the toil of the miners in a nearby colliery known as Fosse 8. From the top of the crassier the Germans had an unrestricted view of the British line below them. A full battalion raid on the German lines by the 2nd Rifle Brigade had been repulsed recently with heavy losses, leaving 2nd RB dead on the German wire, some of whom were still recognisable.

Both Rogerson and Jack comment that the stench of the older corpses in the battalion parapets was distressing, and only reduced slightly by sprinkling them with Chloride of Lime. The sector was very active with daily deaths from telescopic sniping, from Minenwerfer fire, and from mining, often in trenches only a few feet from the enemy. Because of the regular detonation of mines, chalk heaps and craters abounded in no man's land. These were the nightly stage for murderous struggles with trench club, pistol and knife. During the day sentries could not look over the parapet because of the sniping; they could only peer at each other with small periscopes clipped to their bayonet blades.

Rogerson describes a Minenwerfer (Minnie) attack as follows: 'Standing over three feet six inches in height and filled with 200 pounds of explosive, they had a more demoralising effect than any other single form of enemy action. There was no sound of distant discharge. Ears had to be sharp to hear a warning whistle blown by the German gunners before they fired their mortars. Eyes had to be sharp to watch for the shape, which would soar ponderously upward, turn slowly over and over in its downward flight like a tumbler pigeon, and burst with a shattering crash, rending into fragments everything around. Men do not easily throw off the shock of seeing all that could be found of four comrades buried in one ground sheet.' (Abridged).

The 21-year-old Ben Clayton has left no written description of such an experience, but his cartoons are themselves a graphic record of the Minnies, the mining and the rats described in the introductory passages of '12 days on the Somme'. On 12th September, he sketched a West Yorks infantryman with his eyes fixed on an incoming Minnie. The look of horror on the face of the petrified soldier captures the terror described in Rogerson's script.

An incoming Minny

Nine days later, Ben depicts the panic-stricken disarray produced by the impending arrival of a Minnie as three subalterns dive into a deep dugout to avoid it.

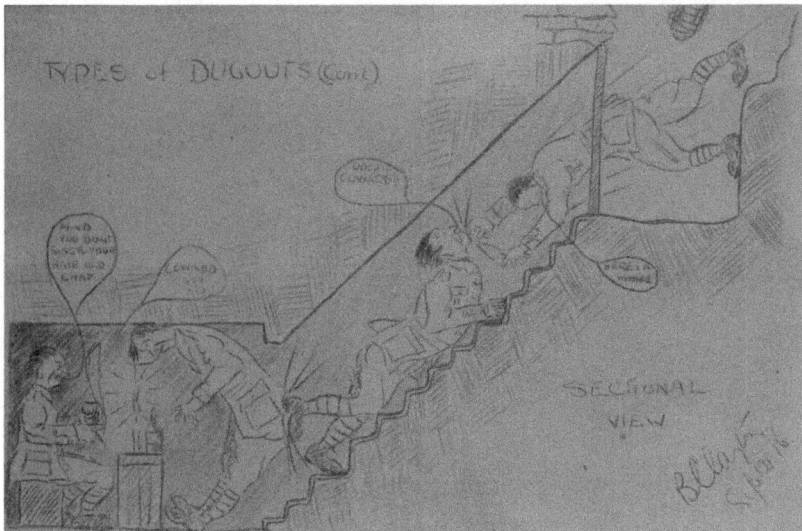

More incoming ordnance

Colonel Jack comments in his diary on 13th September: 'Some of the trenches have been badly mauled by Minenwerfer fire, three men being blown to bits by one bomb. These heavy trench mortar shells, with their terrific explosion, are intensely disagreeable.'

On 13th September, two daredevil enemy raiders crawled across to the West Yorks trenches at nightfall and dispatched two sentries with pistol fire. The same evening Ben produced a sketch entitled 'Home Thoughts From Abroad'. A Second Lieutenant sits under shellfire in a deep dugout illuminated by a single candle; he is sipping 'lime juice (with rum?)' and smoking a cigarette. 'Are we downhearted?' he asks a well-fed rat sitting upright opposite him. 'No!' comes the reply.

Home thoughts from abroad

On 14th September, Ben sketched the first of four more images of daily events in the Loos Salient. Intentionally humorous, but with a more abstruse meaning, the first sketch depicts the panic caused by a pungent odour of rancid cheese. Mistaken by the troops for poisonous gas, the frantic beating of a suspended empty 18-pounder brass shell case sounds the Gas Alarm. A terrified soldier confuses an empty sandbag for his mask and pulls it over his head; he falls to the floor shouting that he is gassed. Another anticipates oblivion as he discovers that the goggles of his gas mask are broken; a third abandons his comrades to hunt for a missing mask.

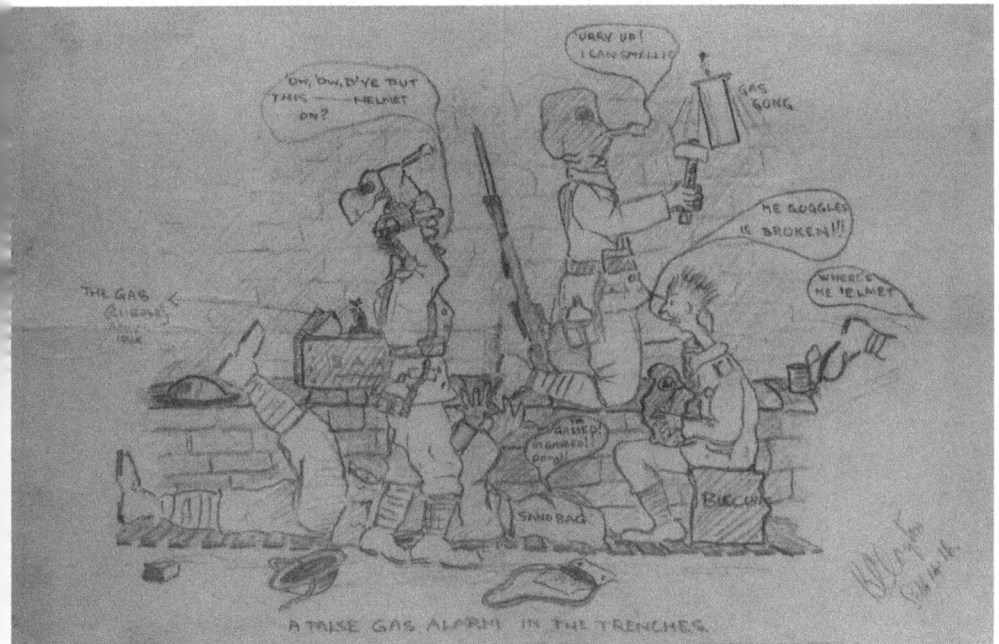

A gas alarm!

'Gas! Gas! Quick, boys – an ecstasy of fumbling,
fit the clumsy helmets just in time.
But someone was yelling out and stumbling.
And floundering like a man in fire or lime.'

Wilfred Owen, 1917.

The second sketch of 14th September portrays a dishevelled and mud-encrusted cook smoking a pipe whilst producing a meal for C Company's Officers. He is frying corned beef rissoles over a coke brazier. In the mess, one subaltern says, 'excellent rissoles old chap' to his dining companion who remarks, 'Just wait until the trifle comes down!'

The Trenchermen

In 'Doubts of Dugouts' sketched three days later, a Second Lieutenant and a Captain are dining underground by candlelight in a dugout labelled 'C Company Headquarters' (Captain Hawley and Second Lieutenant Clayton?). 'I tell you I can hear tapping,' says the subaltern. 'Rot, its only rats,' says the Captain, as a spider lowers itself onto his hot supper, presumably produced by the same cook. In the Von Tirpz (sic) Gallery directly below, a German miner wearing the Iron Cross is using a pickaxe to extend the gallery whilst pleading for silence: 'Quiet be!!' he says, just as his comrade drops a large box of Lyddite and whispers, 'Will it off go?'

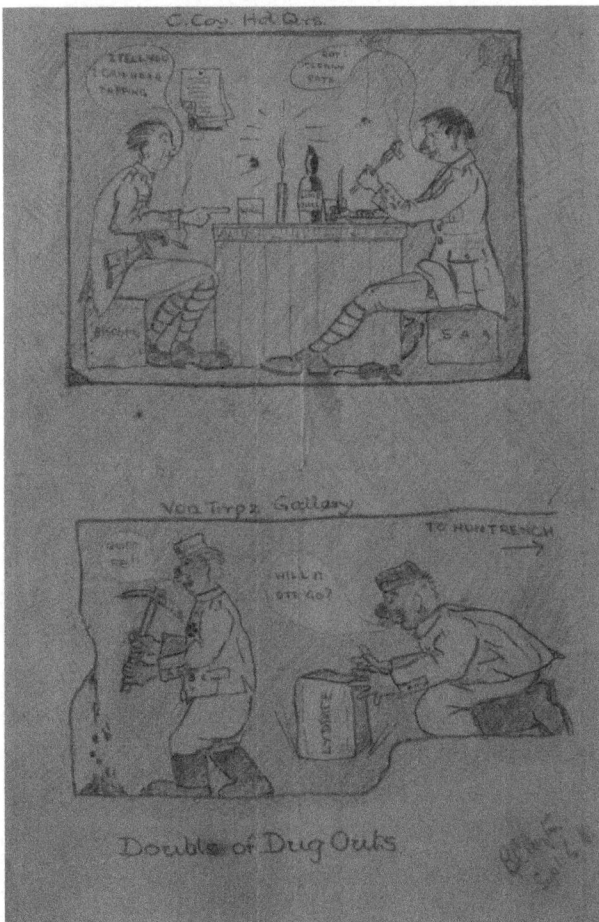

An eventful meal

A fourth sketch from that time is entitled 'Kamerad!!' and depicts the same German soldier complete with Iron Cross, his knees covered with mud from tunnelling, who states 'I haf myself to give up Gome!'

Kamerad!

On 15th September, Second Lieutenants Smailes and Fisher and 24 volunteers from the ranks carried out a trench raid. The purpose of the raid was to secure prisoners for interrogation by the Intelligence Corps. The West Yorks raiders had to make two separate sorties that night, as the first was aborted when the German wire was found intact. Colonel Jack only reluctantly sanctioned a second sortie because the Brigade Commander had ordered the raid. The wire was intact at the second attempt, and the patrol was fired upon. Private Standish was killed and Sergeant Mellor was wounded. The two Subalterns and the Battalion Medical Officer had to return into no-man's land several times before the casualties could be brought into the West Yorks lines.

On 17th September, the battalion went into billets at Labourse between Noeux-les-Mines and Bethune. Colonel Jack's 'Out of the Line' exercises were performed daily by all ranks. Ben depicts officers senior to him undertaking bayonet practice, drill and gymnastics with varying degrees of skill and enthusiasm.

A school for officers

Bayonet practice

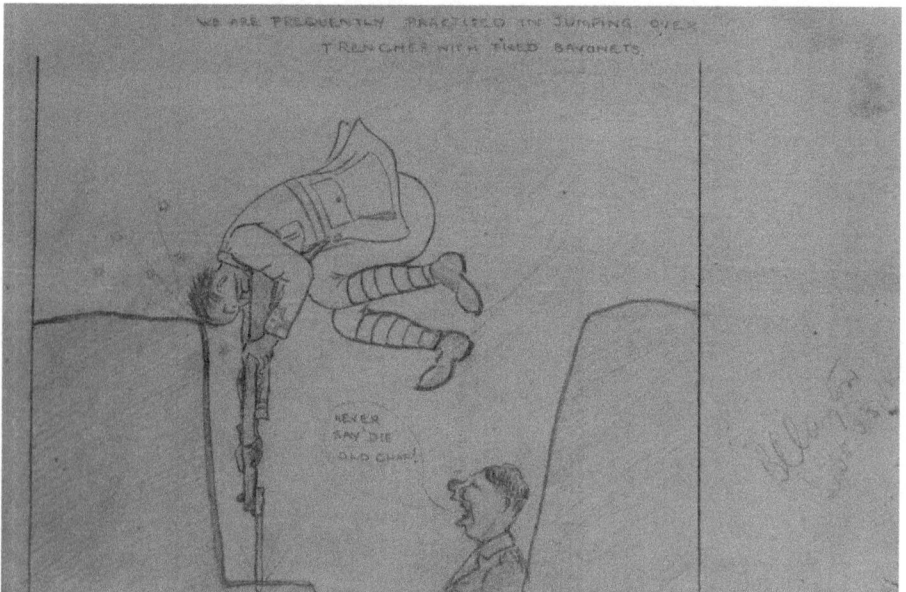

Practice makes perfect

He also sketched his billet in Labourse; unusually luxurious, it is equipped with a mirror that allows him to knot his tie!

Home comforts

Nine days later, the battalion returned to trenches only a few hundred yards from the Hohenzollern Redoubt at Hulluch. A despondent 'New Army' battalion was waiting to be relieved by the 2nd West Yorks who found 'the wire, trenches and men's dugouts were in a shocking state while the officers' dugouts were pretty good,' writes Colonel Jack, adding 'this is a bad sign.' Jack confides, 'There were none of the usual maps, defence orders or store inventories' and that the unit concerned was the worst he had ever relieved.

On 4th October, Ben produced an insight into the mind of every 21-year-old soldier. The sketch is of an encounter, possibly in Bethune, with an attractive young French woman, a professional photographer, who is using a tripod camera in her studio to take his photograph. Ben is in his best uniform, his rank displayed on his sleeve rather than (as was becoming customary because of the cull of subalterns) on his shoulder, and the 'Galloping Horse' cap badge of the West Yorks prominent in his cap. He affects a pair of fashionably baggy jodhpurs disappointingly equipped with puttees rather than leather gaiters, possibly because the latter were not available in provincial France at short notice. He is carrying his officers' walking stick and best leather gloves. 'Regardez moi, monsieur' says the stern but alluring lady. 'Oui, oui, avec plaisir, mademoiselle,' Ben replies with a cheesy smile. A jealous colleague on the landing peers round the door of the studio to give unwanted encouragement. This portrayal of his encounter with an attractive woman, perhaps mutually satisfying to both parties, is the only time the artist allows a frisson of sexuality to enter his sketches.

'Un frisson d'amour'

The onset of autumn ended the battalion's recuperation in Artois. In October the 8th division was transferred back to the Somme as part of the XIV Corps (Lieutenant General Lord Cavan) of General Rawlinson's 4th Army. Lieutenant Colonel Jack records that the 2nd West Yorks had made good use of their time. 'Out of 90 days spent in the Loos Salient after their fearful losses on 1st July, 2nd West Yorkshire has been in the trenches for 70; it is nevertheless in a good state. Discipline and morale are satisfactory … All duties mentioned have been performed for trifling casualties in action…' (Abridged).

CHAPTER NINE

THE SOMME

On 17th October 1916, after a tedious 40-mile journey, partly by train, the battalion marched into billets in Meaulte. Before the war this white-washed village was almost a suburb of Albert and had an attractive cobbled main street, but now it was full of wrecked buildings, with deep, liquid mud intermixed with horse dung on all the roads, and fresh drafts of men and munitions everywhere, all destined for the renewed Somme offensives. The battalion bivouac'd in the remnants of Bernafray Wood in anticipation of a frontal assault at Le Transloy.

Rawlinson's 4th Army had captured three German defensive ridges on the Somme battlefield while the 8th Division was in Artois, but the enemy had constructed three more defensive positions in those three months. The latest British assault had started at the beginning of October 1916 against the next ridge at Le Transloy.

A West Yorks' minimum reserve, consisting of the second in command, Major McLaren, seven other officers, two warrant officers and ten soldiers per company, was sent to the transport lines as a cadre in case the battalion was completely destroyed once again. The battalion, much depleted from its peacetime muster, then marched through the night of 22nd October into Windmill Trench, after an exhausting afternoon moving stores and ammunition.

The weary troops learned only at that stage that they were to be the close support battalion for an attack by two of the other battalions in the 23rd Brigade. Next day, after waiting for the morning mist to lift, the 2nd Scottish Rifles and the 2nd Middlesex Regiment advanced under a covering bombardment to capture part of Zenith trench. The battalions continued for another 200 yards, and occupied Orion Trench, but in the afternoon a counter attack caused a retreat back to Zenith trench. Enemy artillery fire and enfilading machine guns prevented any meaningful advance by the other brigades of the 8th Division. Further assaults were impossible due to the foul weather, the clinging gelatinous mud and the sophistication of the German defensive system.

On 25th October, the 2nd West Yorks were sent forward to relieve the 2nd Scottish Rifles (Cameronians) through a quagmire. Rain, deep mud, shellfire and bullets made the advance long and hazardous. Fortunately there were only 20 casualties. The weather worsened, and with the leading two battalions of 23rd Brigade in such an exposed position in the new salient, the shelling continued. Patrols were sent into no-man's land at dusk to prevent lateral infiltration by enemy raiders and one night 16 prisoners were captured, but the barrage killed three officers, including the doctor and 41 other ranks.

Second Lieutenant Clayton's two sketches from these stressful days reflect the dispiriting circumstances of the battalion. On 24th October he portrays a tented encampment where three soldiers are discussing a 'Blighty Wound'. 'Lucky bloke,' says one envious soldier to a comrade whose right arm is in a sling. 'I say, don't forget th'old pub' says a third in a thick Bradford accent as he peers at them out of his tent.

Blighty Wound

A sketch of 26th October shows Ben in a deep, cold dugout with an empty sandbag wrapped around his feet for warmth, a balaclava on his head, with his badges of rank on his shoulder rather than his sleeve and his Webley revolver hanging on the wall. He is smoking a pipe by the light of a solitary candle, with a rat watching him from the corner. This sketch, 'Getting Up A Fug' probably reflects the experience of 2nd West Yorks in the salient.

The smokehouse

Before the attack on 23rd October, the battalion's ration strength was 437 infantrymen, but in holding the newly won position for eight days, six officers and 214 other ranks were lost, mostly from the endless shelling. On 30th October the despondent battalion went back into Divisional Reserve, at Meaulte. General Rawlinson watched them disengage and records in his diary: 'I met a variety of men coming out of the trenches, stone cold and beat to the world. They were the Devons and West Yorks of the 8th Division … the conditions in the trenches are very bad as men get beat – in certainly 48 hours – under such conditions an offensive does not look hopeful." (Abridged).

The attack on Zenith trench by the 8th Division was judged to be a failure but soon afterwards the equally weary 17th Division attacked through the morning mist without a barrage, and carried the position with the loss of only ten men. The 8th Division was, according to General Rawlinson 'much played out … and I doubt they could be called upon for a successful offensive.' According to their Divisional History, the senior officers and staff were completely exhausted to the point where mail was undelivered and rations were sometimes not sent forward on time. The incidence of trench foot was rising as the weary infantrymen became lackadaisical about wearing dry socks and treating their feet with whale oil; uniforms were muddy, buttons were unpolished, the soldiers were unkempt and some were caught drinking contaminated water from shell holes, the better to contact gastro-enteritis and avoid further front-line service.

After only eight days of rest, the 2nd West Yorks were ordered through the unrelenting deep mud and torrential rain to a bivouac at the apex of the salient opposite the remnants of Le Transloy, close to LesBoeufs Wood. Battalion headquarters, about half a mile behind the front line, was in a recently overrun German trench roofed with corrugated iron, one end being blocked with sandbags against which a stove had been placed. A battalion briefing between the four company commanders and Lieutenant Colonel Jack decided that A and B Companies would go into the front line just over the brow of the Le Transloy ridge, with C (Second Lieutenant Clayton's company) and D companies in support in the valley immediately below the apex of the salient, in Dewdrop Trench. The latter had been a substantial German fortification, but was now a wilderness of deep mud, twisted metal, smashed dugouts and unburied dead.

The weather conditions were atrocious, heavy rain making the ground so deep in mud as to be almost impassable. After five days, C and D Companies joined A and B Companies in the front line for 24 hours as General Gough's 5th Army in the neighbouring sector launched an attack. The battalion was able to witness another assault on Beaumont-Hamel, still in German hands five months after the failure to capture the village on 1st July. Beaumont-Hamel was eventually taken by 51st Division in appalling conditions in the middle of November.

The exhausted 2nd West Yorks were relieved before then and spent a few more days in reserve, labouring yet again under the direction of the Royal Engineers.

On 19th November, they were transported by train to Le Fay, a brick built hamlet near Oisemont, 20 miles south west of Amiens, a serene part of La France Profonde far from the Somme battlefield. There 2nd West Yorks received drafts of 451 more men, about half their peacetime muster, and experienced a glorious five weeks of rest, recreation, re-equipment and training. Ben sketched a self-portrait of himself in 'A First day in Rest' that sums up his delight. He is asleep in a real bed with bedclothes around him, a dreamy smile on his resting features. Tins of tobacco and a pipe surround him for the morning.

Out of the line

On 15th November Colonel Jack records in his diary: 'All ranks are expected to shave daily, even in the trenches, but this order is relaxed when conditions are extremely bad.'

On 21st November, Ben sketched a second self-portrait of himself sitting on his military trunk, shaving in front of a small mirror. A smoking brazier is cooking the contents of a tin can that has been partly opened with a tin opener. The can's label is not decipherable, but is probably Maconochie's Stew, a watery Aberdonian concoction of beans, sliced potatoes and carrots, occasionally flavoured with sparse quantities of onions and meat. Ben is now wearing a pair of knee-length boots. These are probably standard issue rubber gumboots, notorious for producing trench foot when wet socks were worn with them, rather than officers' knee-length leather boots.

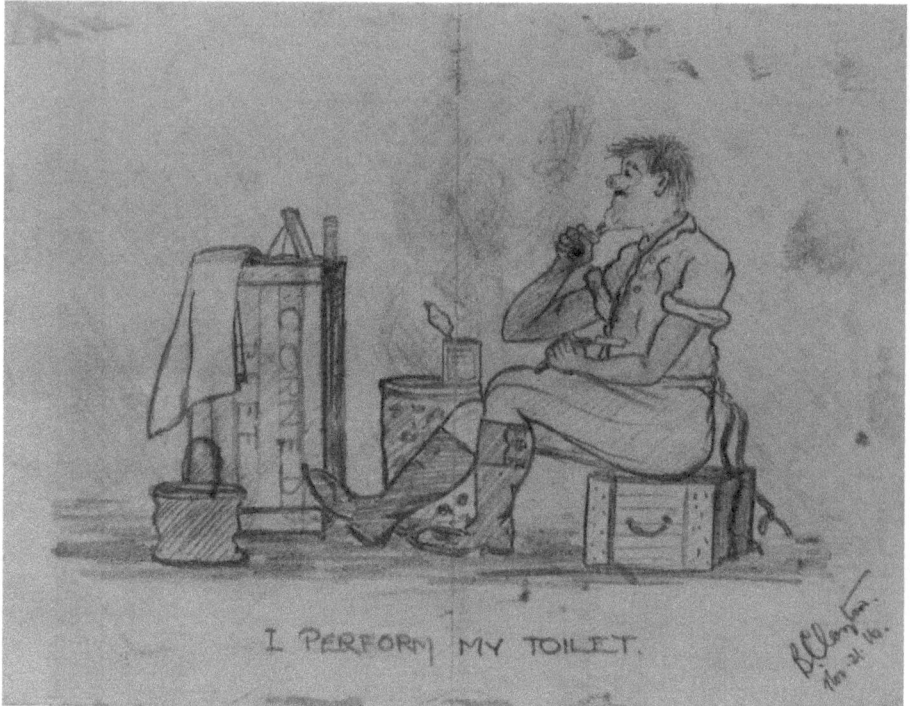

I PERFORM MY TOILET.

'There is no need to live like a pig even if surrounded by filth.'

On 6th December 1916, during 2nd West Yorks' time in Le Fay, the Liberal Prime Minister, Mr H H Asquith had resigned, as the Cabinet no longer had confidence in his ability to prosecute the War. Asquith was replaced by David Lloyd George, a more effective War Leader, whose appointment irrevocably split the Liberal Party. The new Prime Minister rejected tentative enemy proposals about peace talks but acquiesced to the continuation of the attritional campaign on the Somme.

All too soon, the rest period at Le Fay ended, and 2nd West Yorks returned to the Somme valley for a third time. On 2nd January 1917 they were to the west of Rancourt at Priez Farm, relieving 1st Somerset Light Infantry (SLI) in the front line. An officer of 1st SLI described their trenches at the time as follows: 'The conditions beggar description, the trenches are flooded and have fallen in. There is no cover and the men are being evacuated sick with frost bite and exhaustion by the hundred.' (Abridged from War Diary of 1st S.L.I.).

The 2nd West Yorks went into Brigade Reserve on 6th January and thereafter were employed in working parties in comfortless reserve camps for a month or so, as they were being critically assessed by the new Commanding Officer of 8th Division.

The 4th Army Command had been concerned that the 8th Division under Major General Hudson had not fulfilled its potential since the Battle of Neuve Chapelle in March 1915. In December 1916 an exacting Canadian officer with a cold manner, Major General W G Heneker, suddenly replaced Hudson. Heneker proceeded to conduct a number of critical inspections of 8th Division. Over a three-month period he removed all three of the Brigade Commanders, the Commander of 23rd Brigade, Brigadier General Fagan being replaced in March by Lieutenant Colonel G Grogan. An old colleague of Heneker's from pre-war days in West Africa, Grogan was to win the Victoria Cross on the Aisne in 1918 as a Brigadier General, repeating the achievement of another 8th Division Brigadier General, Brigadier General Coffin, who was awarded the VC at Passchendaele in 1917.

Three of the battalion commanders in 23rd Brigade lost their commands, but Lieutenant Colonel Jack was identified as the senior officer who had been uniquely effective in the Brigade. His ability to foster discipline and spirit in his battalion, as demonstrated by the success of his formal 'Out of the Trenches' routine and by the success of the daredevil raiding parties led by Lieutenant Matthew McConville was acknowledged by Major General Heneker. Jack was to remain in command of 2nd West Yorks until severely wounded by shellfire at Passchendaele and evacuated to England.

The 2nd West Yorks Adjutant, Captain Palmes, fell foul of Heneker at his first encounter because he was unaware of the site of the latrines in a camp occupied only that day by the battalion; he very narrowly avoided being sent home. On 11th March, Jack records that he had received a 'frigid letter' from division headquarters two weeks beforehand about the 'unacceptable' incidence of trench foot in the 2nd West Yorks. The condition could be checked by obsessive foot hygiene, and was seen by the High Command as a marker for the relationship between other ranks and junior officers. Colonel Jack comments that a lack of care may have been partly responsible, but writes:

'The difficulties of infantry companies do not appear to be fully realised in High Circles, few of whom come to see for themselves the appalling conditions in the trenches, especially during reliefs in glue-like mud and under shell fire. Too often impracticable orders are issued ...' (Abridged).

This was written just after the 2nd West Yorks had completed five days in the trenches at Bouchavesnes. The German line, 150 yards away, was once again above them. The British trenches were thigh deep in mud and liquid slurry. Dugouts could not be constructed because of the flooding. Enemy snipers were very active, so visits to the front line by battalion headquarters were impossible during daylight.

The 2nd West Yorks again supported an attack by other battalions of the 8th Division. This was deemed a success but 1,000 British soldiers were killed or wounded. 2nd West Yorks lost three officers and 80 infantrymen in their subsidiary role, although 217 prisoners were taken 'of less than normal German physique'.

Ben Clayton produced two sketches in January 1917 graphically recording the unhappy situation of the battalion during their third campaign on the Somme. Both portray shell holes being used as advanced observation posts. In the first an officer is sitting below ground level on the edge of a flooded shell hole surrounded by barbed wire, with a waterproof rubber cape around his shoulders. The rain is pouring down. Beneath the cape the officer (Ben?) is writing his report by pencil in a notebook.

Ground Zero on the Somme

In the second sketch an infantryman is sitting in a shell hole smoking a pipe; his back is to the enemy as he surveys the enemy trenches through a periscope fixed to his bayonet. A British shell passes overhead on its way to the enemy line. The sentry wears thigh-length gumboots, gloves and a balaclava beneath his steel helmet; boxes of hand grenades surround him.

Ben comments: 'Dugouts nil, trench boards ditto. sandbags ditto. Rations nappoo. Water shell hole, mud beaucoup'.

Periscope duty on the Somme

These realistic scenes must be his recollections of the Battle of Transloy; Colonel Jack records in the entry in his diary of 26th October: 'There are no dugouts in the forward area … officers and men have no cover from the frightful weather except their waterproof sheets.' (Abridged).

The last sketch of January 1917 is a self-portrait. Ben portrays himself as a second lieutenant in a waterproof trench coat smoking a pipe, relaxed and at ease, some way from the War. Entitled 'Dear Mater' and dated 18/1/17, it contains the following message to Isabel Clayton: 'still keeping fit, no time to write, love to all', surely proof that a powerful mother-and-son relationship had developed between Ben and Isabel in the 15 years since John Clayton's second marriage.

Dear Mater

Isabella Clayton, 1917

In March 1917 Ben sketched 'The Latest Thing in Uhlans', probably a portrayal of the episode in the attack at Bouchavesnes where '217 prisoners of less than normal good German physique were brought in'. The sketch depicts a very young, very nervous and very small German soldier, complete with a coalscuttle helmet, who is very keen to surrender to a taller, urbane British infantryman.

'Kamerad!!!' cries the 'Prospective Hun Prisoner', extending a hopeful right hand. 'That's orl right', says Tommy, smoking a downturned pipe with his rifle and fixed bayonet slung over his shoulder', but where 'ave yer left yer rattle?'

Tommy's cockney accent seems to indicate a Londoner of the 2nd Middlesex (one of the attacking battalions) rather than a man from the West Riding of Yorkshire.

An 'Uhlan' surrenders

CHAPTER TEN
ADVANCE TO THE HINDENBURG LINE

By 13th March Ben Clayton had been promoted Lieutenant and was in command of B Company. On the night of 14th March he volunteered to lead a trench raid. These hazardous affairs often produced British casualties. The raiders, all volunteers, blackened their faces, covered their boots with wash-leathers the better to deaden footsteps and armed themselves with pistols, knobkerries, knives and hand grenades. They crawled out on all fours into no man's land in groups of ten or more, led by a subaltern. Their intention was to penetrate the German wire and, unseen, enter a German trench. The mission was to kill or capture as many of the enemy as possible and return unharmed. Many seasoned infantrymen saw trench raids as unnecessary, but senior officers, rarely leaders of such sorties, were keen to establish local ascendancy over the enemy.

At dusk on the day of the raid an alert sentry noticed through his periscope that the trenches opposite seemed deserted. Scouting parties encountered no opposition. At 8 p.m. B and C Companies advanced unhindered into Drossen Trench. The German Army was retreating into the Hindenburg line (Siegfried Position), a defence system between Arras and Soissons often more than 20 miles behind the previous German positions.

Withdrawal to the Hindenburg Line

Siegfriedstellung had been prepared by the German general staff over the previous six months to allow elastic defence in depth. Reverse slope deep trenches, underground fortresses and 'pillbox' machine gun emplacements of reinforced concrete had been constructed and were cross-referenced for artillery and machine-gun support behind mile after mile of dense barbed wire. The number of divisions necessary to hold the shortened line was thus reduced; German losses on the Somme, at Verdun and against the Brusilov Offensive on the Eastern Front had been heavy.

The planned withdrawal was named Operation Alberich (Alberichbewegung) after the malicious dwarf in the Nibelung Saga.

Anything of value was destroyed by the troops as they withdrew. Roads, railways and bridges, domestic buildings, orchards and crops were all laid waste. French civilians were used as construction labourers and then transported eastward. The wasteland was amply supplied with booby traps to impede the ultra cautious Allied advance. This was spearheaded by a cavalry screen of mounted yeomanry behind which 2nd West Yorks warily and rather ineptly followed the Germans up the Somme valley to Nurlu. Warfare in the open was a novel experience for British soldiers after two years below ground. Lieutenant Colonel Jack describes how the 1914 'mobile war' lessons of movement, fire and communication had to be rediscovered. Three days were wasted constructing defensive trenches in the sleet on the apex of Nurlu ridge at a time when continuation of the advance might have been rewarding.

Twenty-four hours later, Brigadier General Grogan apologetically informed Jack that 'Higher Command' were dissatisfied with the lack of push of the infantry. Jack was exasperated. The 2nd West Yorks had been cautioned twice that they had advanced too far and too fast for their own safety; for 72 hours they had been held up digging defences when they could have pushed on. Later that day the battalion relieved the 2nd Middlesex and, at Jack's urging, advanced rapidly a mile or so beyond the Middlesex's outposts until they were only 1,000 yards from the enemy pickets in Heudicourt.

On 8th March, Revolution had broken out in Russia. Seven days later the Tsar resigned but the replacement liberal government pledged to continue the fight against Germany. On 8th April, unrestricted submarine warfare and the leak by Great Britain of the coded Zimmermann Telegram from Germany to Mexico proposing an alliance, caused the United States of America to enter the War on the side of the Allies as an 'Associate Power'.

On 9th April, Germany facilitated Lenin's journey from exile in Zurich to St Petersburg. Within eight months the Bolsheviks had supplanted the unstable liberal regimes and Russia had sued for peace. German troops on the Eastern Front were then able to transfer westward the better to replenish their manpower deficit on the Western Front.

From 9th April until 16th May, the British 1st and 3rd Armies fought the Battle of Arras to the north of 8th Division's position. The Canadians took Vimy Ridge, but further advance proved too costly against the sophisticated German strategy of exponential defence in depth. The frontal assaults of the British infantry gradually petered out into another stalemate.

On 12th April, a month after the onset of mobile warfare on the Somme battlefield, the 2nd West Yorks were on the outskirts of Villers-Guislain, a village in front of Siegfriedstellung near Cambrai. The battalion attacked in a snowstorm with the prevailing wind behind them. B Company advanced up an open slope in two ranks, just behind D Company, until both were checked by machine-gun fire in front of a thick belt of uncut wire.

The 2nd West Yorks achieved its objectives on the outskirts of the village, but the uncut wire caused Colonel Jack to recommend postponement of the advance of the 2nd Battalion of the Devonshire Regiment into Villers-Guislain the following morning. Brigadier General Grogan rejected his advice. The attack of the 2nd Devonshires was held up on the uncut wire and many West Country soldiers were killed by Spandau fire. On 18th April, 2nd West Yorks was ordered to take the village, the wire having been cut by high explosive bombardment. The four companies advanced through another fortuitous snowstorm and within an hour had overrun Villers-Guislain. 2nd West Yorks continued to advance half a mile past the village, a mile from their start point. There were only 11 casualties; 18 prisoners and five machine guns were taken.

Colonel Jack attributed his success to the strict discipline of the 2nd West Yorks, to careful training and to minute preparation. He records his praise for the dash, determination and quick bold decisions of all ranks, led by Captain Palmes, still with the battalion despite his excoriating encounter with Major General Heneker. A reconnoitre of the captured salient by Jack and Palmes allowed them to confirm the thickness of the wire belt protecting Siegfriedstellung about two miles away.

Ten days in the divisional reserve followed. Colonel Jack's 'Out of the Line' Exercises were continued, and some leave in Paris was available for deserving officers. On 4th May, the battalion was back in the line in front of Siegfriedstellung at Gouzeaucourt. Ben Clayton sketched himself asleep in a brick-lined dugout with his orderly reporting that the enemy were shelling. 'I can't hear them,' says Ben, 'Go away.' Neither Lieutenant Clayton nor a large rat sitting upright behind his bed seems fazed by the shells crashing into the sandbags just above them. The orderly's discomposure may be due to lack of confidence in the strength of his own dugout. The sketch is probably a record of the heavy counter-bombardment of 2nd West York's positions at 4.15 a.m. that morning; three British soldiers were killed and four were wounded. At the time the ration strength of the 2nd West Yorks was only 27 officers and 445 other ranks, half its peacetime muster.

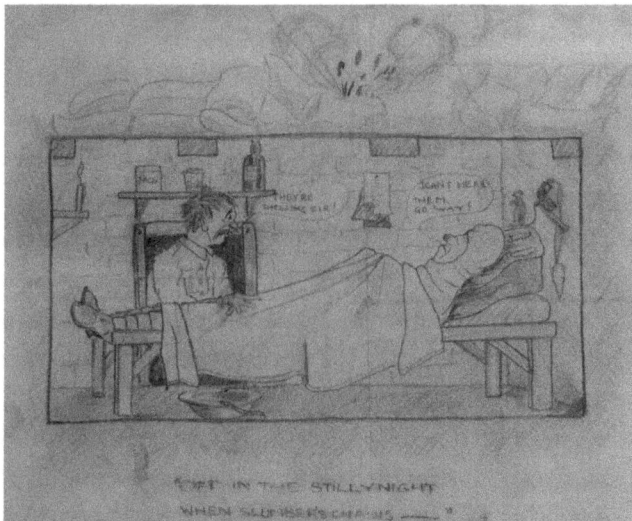

Slumber disturbed

Contemporaneous French attacks under General Nivelle further south in Champagne, had produced huge losses. On 3rd May, a number of units of the French Army, war weary and possibly inspired by the news from Russia, refused to obey their orders. The shattered Poilus asserted that they would defend their positions but would not advance into interlocking machine-gun fire. Over the next month the mutiny spread throughout the French trenches, forcing the British to continue with attacks all along their line. Senior British officers were aware that these must fail because the bulk of the heavy artillery was still dug in around Arras, but for political reasons the attacks were continued, causing the death of many more British infantrymen.

On 4th May, 2nd West Yorks took over the front line from companies of the 2nd Middlesex and the 2nd Scottish Rifles to allow these battalions to attack the outlying German position at La Vacquerie, a fortified hamlet between Gouzeaucourt and the main defences of the Hindenburg line. A few Germans were killed and about 15 prisoners were taken, but British casualties were considerable. The raid had actually been conceived as an attack to capture and hold La Vacquerie, but when it failed to do so, it was relabelled

The enemy discerningly reported that a 'futile attack' had been repulsed. The Germans continued to bombard the British trenches in front of La Vacquerie for days afterwards, sometimes with gas shells. The 2nd West Yorks remained around Gouzeaucourt for another ten days, in and out of the front line, with snipers and Lewis gunners forward in shell-holes by day and fighting patrols out in no man's land by night, often with fatigue parties simultaneously repairing trench palisades in the darkness. Lieutenant Clayton sketched himself doing his rounds in the front-line trenches and reassuring a newly drafted sentry with bayonet fixed, who could hear Germans talking nearby. The officer still has his rank on his sleeve, and carries a walking stick in spite of recommendations after the Somme battle that officers should be indistinguishable from other ranks, and should have their badges of rank on their shoulders.

Unsettling sounds

The battalion eventually left the front on 14th May and marched 18 miles down the hard won desolation of the Somme battlefield to the unspoilt flood plain of the river. 'Out of the Line' parades and sports days were enlivened by swimming parties in the lagoons of the lazy waterway, producing scenes redolent of those described by Sebastian Faulks in 'Birdsong'. Ben Clayton was promoted to Captain in May 1917. On 1st June, the 2nd West Yorks entrained for the new military station in Bailleul, the Duke of York Station, in anticipation of action in the Ypres Salient.

CHAPTER ELEVEN

THE YPRES SALIENT

'I am not prepared to accept the position of a butcher's boy driving cattle to the slaughter.'

David Lloyd George,
Prime Minister of Great Britain and Ireland,
February 1917.

'What passing-bells for those who die like cattle?
Only the monstrous anger of the guns.
Only the stuttering rifles rapid rattle
Can patter out their hasty orisons.'

(Abridged) Wilfred Owen, October 1917

Ypres (in truth, Ieper) is 25 miles from the coast and acted as a pivot for the British armies in the Great War. If it fell, the French channel ports would be vulnerable, and resupply might depend upon ports on the Bay of Biscay. Two earlier enemy assaults, First Ypres in 1914 and Second Ypres in 1915, had been frustrated but the Germans had seized the higher ground around the city in a 320 degree arc; their commanding view meant that they had possessed the military initiative ever since. All front-line combatants viewed a posting to the Ypres Salient with apprehension because heavy casualties accrued even in the quietest of months.

In January 1917, Field Marshall Haig planned a massive frontal attack from the salient, supposedly to seize the nearby Belgian coastal ports and so deny their use to German submarines returning from the Atlantic. The Royal Navy was losing the battle with the U-boats at the time so the British War Cabinet acquiesced to Haig's plan.

Heavy casualties were inevitable, as Haig's veiled intention was to continue with his policy of manpower attrition. This strategy seemed tenable to Headquarters staff because tanks and ground attack aircraft were in their infancy as weapons of war and a decisive breakthrough by infantry alone seemed increasingly unlikely against the sophisticated fixed defences of the enemy.

Bailleul became a huge base surrounded by concealed supply dumps for the growing number of British troops in the salient. Multiple railways led from Bailleul to Ypres, with tramways from the railheads up to the forward distribution areas. Artillery, shells, mortars, machine guns and their ammunition were transported forward nightly.

To neuter Haig's strategy, two German General Staff officers, Major Bauer and Captain Geyer, had produced 'Conduct of the Defensive Battle in Positional Warfare' in December 1916. This emphasises the principle of an elastic defence in depth, with front-line trenches being thinly manned.

'Principles of Field Fortifications', published slightly later, recommends that zigzag communication trenches, running up from the rear, should interlock with the forward transverse fighting trenches, thus forming a grid pattern. These communication trenches allowed the swift advance of 'Sturmtruppen' from behind the front line to any grid point on the map. Each grid was cross-targeted by fixed machine guns from neighbouring grids and by artillery from behind the line. The deeper the advance of the enemy, the more vigorous the reaction of the local commander who could trigger a sequential triple response of machine guns, artillery and assault troops.

Each grid contained at least one reinforced concrete pillbox ('Mebus' – Mannschafts Eisenbeton Unterstande), equipped with machine guns. The pillbox was heavily fortified towards the enemy line but had little fortification to the rear. If taken, it would be of minimal value to the attacking troops. Farms were turned into fortresses reinforced with concrete palisades up to five feet thick that could withstand a direct hit from an 18-pounder artillery shell.

The system was designed to stop each frontal attack in a killing field in front of a fortress, there to be broken up by Spandau fire and bombardment, followed by a counter-attack from the rear by rested and specially trained Eingraf infantry. Around the salient there were five more defensive lines in addition to the front trenches, all protected by dense wire and stretching back some six miles. The German Army fought for their front trenches, but not necessarily in them.

For two months the 2nd West Yorks familiarised themselves with the Ypres Salient, sometimes stationed underground at Ypres in the catacombs beneath Vauban's 17th-century ramparts, sometimes in Army Reserve, where in June 1917 they observed the relative success of General Plumer's Battle of Messines Ridge, notable for the destruction caused by explosive mines detonated under the German front line. Sometimes they were further back, near St Omer, where they practised coordinating frontal assaults with creeping artillery barrages.

Twice they were in the front trenches southeast of Ypres in the Belwaarde Farm Sector near Hooge, the site of two savage battles in 1915 during Second Ypres. It was here that Captain Clayton drew his last sketch. Entitled 'I am once more in the Trenches' and subtitled 'je m'ennui' ('I am bored') it depicts a moustachioed young infantry officer standing on duckboards in a waterproof trench coat in the rain, with water dripping off the coat onto the duckboards. Ben has his hands in his pockets close to a webbing holster that contains his pistol. He has a knapsack on his back and a walking stick under his left arm. The trench is named 'Brewery Lane', and seems deep and well revetted with sandbags to protect against incoming shellfire. A dugout is visible in the forward wall of the trench, as are the butt of a rifle and a box of hand grenades. The summer monsoon that was to have such an effect on the Battle of Passchendaele has clearly begun.

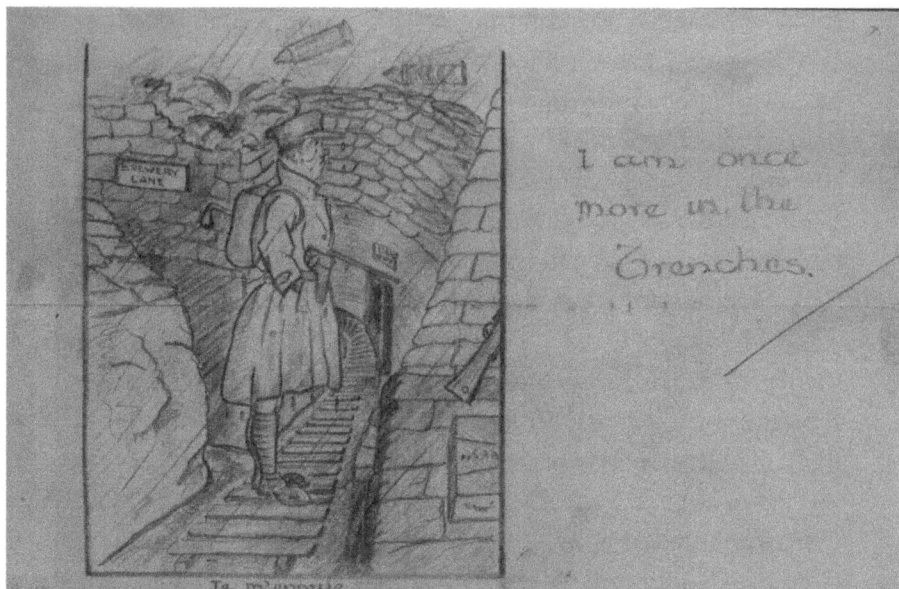

'Je m'ennuie'

The Battle of Messines Ridge was carried out by General Plumer, the Commander of the salient for two years. By capturing and holding Messines Ridge he ensured that an attack on Ypres from the higher ground on the most southwesterly border of the salient was henceforth impossible.

Three days later, Plumer was ready to renew his advance, to 'bite and hold' some of the higher land to the southeast, on the Gheluvelt Plateau. With the forces at his disposal he could not guarantee a successful advance to Passchendaele Ridge three miles away, so he was ordered to consolidate.

The task of a rapid advance towards Passchendaele was given to General Gough of 5th Army, the Army to which the 2nd West Yorks belonged, as part of the 23rd Brigade of the 8th Division, II Corps (Lieutenant General Jacob). The delay in renewing the battle while the enemy was disorganised was a major factor in the subsequent slaughter, as the German Staff anticipated the site of the next attack and spent the available time strengthening defences.

Gough was the youngest of Haig's Generals. From an Irish Protestant military family, three of his closest relatives had received the Victoria Cross. This may have contributed to his reputation amongst his soldiers as a hot-headed officer with little regard for the lives of his troops. His plan of attack was disrupted by the summer monsoon depicted by Captain Clayton. The relentless rain soon turned the brooks on the low-lying polders east of Ypres into torrents. A lengthy preliminary bombardment by the British artillery destroyed this ancient drainage system and produced broad lagoons of gelatinous mud over much of the battlefield, interspersed with flooded shell holes.

On higher ground near the south-eastern boundary of the salient, the enemy were in possession of a series of woods and copses given names by the British at the start of the conflict. Trees in Inverness Copse, Nonne Boschen (Nun's Wood), Glencourse Wood and Polygon Wood had been destroyed by British shellfire, but the residual undergrowth had been fortified by the Mebus System. Pillboxes had been constructed from interlocking concrete blocks that were secured with steel rods driven ten feet into the sedge through holes in the blocks; each pillbox contained multiple machine guns. Their position meant that any battalion of the 8th Division that advanced from the Belwaarde Farm sector north eastward across the flooded polders towards Zonnebeke and Passchendaele Ridge would be enfiladed, first from the south, and later, as it pushed forward, from the rear.

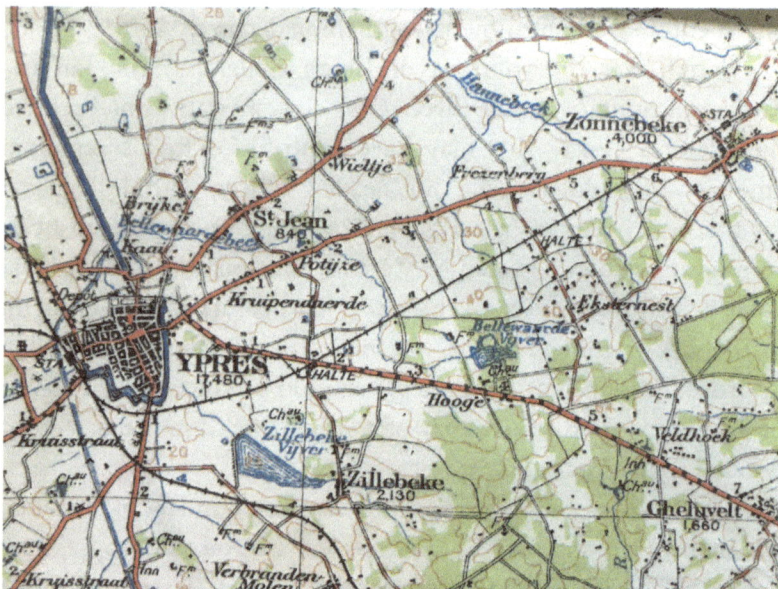

Zonnebeke Battlefield. Ordnance Survey 1916. Polygon Wood is the larger of the woods on the right-hand boundary of the map

Major-General Heneker, Commanding Officer of 8th Division, identified the problem on the 12th August. He submitted that capture of the woods was essential before an advance could be contemplated across the polders, and that sufficient troops and batteries of heavy artillery should be allocated specifically for this task. General Gough rejected the submission.

To the north of the battlefield the Germans had fortified the railway embankment of the Ypres-Rouler railway that ran eastwards about a mile from the northern boundary of the woods. Communication tunnels had been driven through the embankment so that pillboxes north of the embankment could, on instruction, drench an advance along the south side with elevated, indirect Spandau fire.

On 31st July, the 24th and 23rd Brigades of the 8th Division, the latter including the 2nd West Yorks, advanced just before dawn from Belwaarde Farm, their objective being to occupy Westhoek Ridge.

Major McLaren, Captain Clayton and 80 other ranks had presciently been sent to the transport lines in the rear as a 'Minimum Reserve', in case the battalion was wiped out yet again.

A shell buried Lieutenant Colonel Jack as he was in the act of returning to his battalion headquarters after cheering his men forward with his hunting horn; he was evacuated from the field. Major McLaren was summoned and became the Commanding Officer of the 2nd West Yorks. The attack, led by Captain Palmes, soon bogged down and, as anticipated by Heneker, was enfiladed from the left, from the right, and from the rear by machine guns and artillery fire.

It was in these circumstances that Brigadier Coffin of the 24th Brigade of 8th Division was awarded the Victoria Cross. Sturmtruppen counter-attacked and few of the initial gains were held. Out of the 16 officers and 600 other ranks of the 2nd West Yorks who advanced that day, 10 officers and 209 other ranks were casualties. Major McLaren and Captain Palmes were among the dead. Major H St J Jeffries of the neighbouring Worcestershire Regiment was detailed to become the new Commanding Officer.

After relief, the survivors marched back to Halifax Camp between Poperinghe and Ypres. Major General Heneker congratulated them on their steadfast performance. Next day the remnants of the battalion proceeded to nearby Dominion Camp where once again they were congratulated, this time by Lieutenant General Jacob.

Over the next 14 days, fresh drafts were received but Matthew McCormick finally left to join the Royal Flying Corps, and Captain Clayton's contemporary, who had advanced on 31st July, Captain Ingham, went on leave. Ben Clayton was thus the most senior officer trained by Lieutenant Colonel Jack still to be serving with the 2nd West Yorks. A Captain Baker joined from the neighbouring 2nd Middlesex to replace Captain Palmes.

Under Major Jeffries, Lieutenant Colonel Jack's 'Out of the Line' routines were resumed. Afternoon classes in musketry, bombing and use of both the medium and light machine guns followed morning drill under the Sergeant Major. Westhoek Ridge was eventually secured on the 8th August, so a second attack by the 8th Division was planned north-eastwards across the polders. The 23rd and 24th Brigades practised a further advance behind a creeping bombardment and revised their methods of holding captured ground.

The two brigades divided into platoons and marched undetected to Swan Château, just south of Ypres, and to the west of Zillebeke. Officers from each company went forward to reconnoitre the topography eastwards from Westhoek Ridge to their objective, Anzac Ridge, two miles away with the heavily fortified farm, the Zonnebeke Redoubt (Odin Redoubt to the Germans), on its crest.

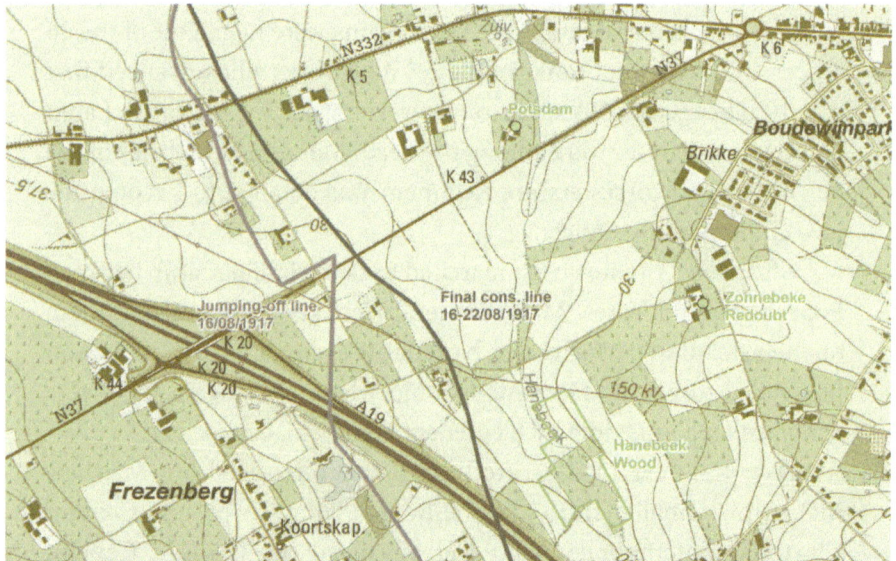

Modern map of Zonnebeke Battlefield, 2017. The N37 follows the bed of the old railway line. [Kindly donated by Simon Augustyn of the Passchendaele Memorial Museum at Zonnebeke.]

At 4.45 a.m. on the 16th August, the second attack of the 8th Division at the Battle of Passchendaele was undertaken by the 23rd Brigade on the left and the 25th Brigade on the right.

In the 23rd Brigade ten officers and four hundred other ranks were available in the depleted 2nd West Yorks. They were to the right of the 2nd Middlesex, who advanced from Railway Wood, a wood close to Belwaarde Farm, north-eastwards along the south side of the Ypres-Roulers railway embankment.

C Company of 2nd West Yorks was immediately to the right of 2nd Middlesex, B Company was the middle company, and A Company was alongside the 25th Brigade troops to their right. The infantry attack was coordinated with a creeping bombardment of the flooded polders by one hundred and eighty 18-pounder field guns, equivalent to the enemy 'whizz bangs', and seventy two howitzers, equivalent to the enemy 'Jack Johnsons'. The barrage crept forward 100 yards every five minutes, thus giving the attackers time to 'bite and hold' the land they were newly occupying.

The enemy held the northern side of the railway embankment and were simultaneously attacked there by troops from the 16th Division, the Division from Catholic Ireland under Major General William Hickie. These soldiers had been the pre-war 'Irish Volunteers', formed to counteract the Protestant 'Ulster Volunteers', as Civil War had loomed in 1914 after the passage of the Irish Home Rule Act. At the outbreak of the Great War, the Irish Volunteers had joined the British Army en masse to defend another small Catholic nation, Belgium.

On the right of the sodden battlefield the Germans still held the high woods on the south-eastern boundary of the salient so, again, as on 31st July, the advancing Brigades of the 8th Division were to be enfiladed from the right at the beginning of their attack and from the rear as the attack proceeded. To stop this process the 56th London Division was given the difficult task of seizing Glencourse Wood, Inverness Copse, Nonne Boschen and part of Polygon Wood.

Both Brigades of the 8th Division followed the barrage across the flooded shell craters and muddy lagoons of the battlefield. After leaving Railway Wood, the two battalions of 23rd Brigade entered Hanebeek Wood where a brace of German machine guns was captured. They crossed the swollen Hanebeek on portable bridges and continued up the gentle slope towards the Zonnebeke Redoubt on Anzac Ridge, the 2nd Middlesex on the left being continually held up by concrete fortifications in the railway embankment.

Attack on Zonnebeke, 1917 [from Illustrated London News]

Hanebeek Brook, 16/8/2017

Both battalions of the 23rd Brigade were being drenched by elevated machine-gun fire from over the embankment, as the 16th Division had been unable to silence them and tunnels in the embankment allowed easy communication between the various groups of Spandau gunners. Ominously, a flattened area, 400 yards square, around the Zonnebeke Redoubt had been prepared as a zoned killing field.

The 2nd West Yorks captured the Zonnebeke Redoubt

Die Fernfprechvermittlung „Odin" bei Zonnebeke   Gefr. Ellerbrock

Zonnebeke Redoubt, 1917

before 7 a.m. on 16th August. By 7.30 a.m. the survivors of the battalion had advanced a short distance past the Redoubt towards Zonnebeke, where they attempted to consolidate. Unfortunately, the 2nd Middlesex was still held up alongside the railway embankment and the 25th Brigade was unable to advance because it was being continuously enfiladed by the Polygon Wood machine guns, still unsuppressed by the 56th Division.

The 2nd West Yorks was thus dangerously exposed from its left, right, front and rear, at the very tip of a narrow salient. At 8.30 a.m. the battalion became the principal targets of Spandau and artillery fire, deliberately directed onto the prepared killing field. The 2nd West Yorks was soon forced to retreat back to the western side of Anzac Ridge in front of the Zonnebeke Redoubt. Enemy infantry then counter-attacked and the survivors were pushed back to Hanebeek Wood.

Captain Clayton was badly wounded in the action and, being

incapable of retreat, was left behind near the Redoubt. At 3.30 p.m.
Hanebeek Wood was penetrated from the rear by enemy infantry
from Polygon Wood. The 2nd West Yorks were unable to call up a
satisfactory bombardment by the use of their flares and pigeons, and
so had to retreat back into Railway Wood, where at 8 p.m. the 2nd
Scottish Rifles relieved them.

The attack had been a complete failure. The German system of
flexible defence in depth and counter-attack (Gegenangriff) was
outstandingly successful. The advance of the 23rd and 25th Brigades
towards Zonnebeke on 16th August stands comparison with a more
famous forlorn hope, Pickett's Charge at the Battle of Gettysburg, but
the atrocious weather, the flooded state of the battlefield, the lack of
a reliable system of communication and the bravery of a steadfast
enemy made the task of the British soldiers the more difficult. When
the 16th Division and the 56th Division were unable to achieve their
objectives, success became impossible. Casualties in the 2nd West
Yorks consisted of ten officers and 294 other ranks out of the 400
who attacked. All ten officers were killed including Captain Benjamin
Chipchase Clayton, a Methodist art teacher from County Durham.

CHAPTER TWELVE

REQUIEM

Lying wounded in a wet polder on a prepared killing field in front of the Zonnebeke Redoubt, Ben Clayton was either killed by the Sturmtruppen in their counter-attack or died from his wounds at about 9.30 a.m. on Thursday 16th August 1917.

He was 22 years old and would not have been 23 until 27th May 1918. He was reported 'missing in action' to the battalion adjutant by the few survivors of the 2nd West Yorks after their relief by the 2nd Scottish Rifles at 8 p.m. that night. The efficiency of the General Post Office telegraph system ensured a telegram was delivered to Edmondsley Post Office on Saturday 18th August. Ben's family was informed by the dreaded knock of the telegram boy on the front door at School House.

John Clayton's first action was to collect the family and conduct a prayer meeting for Ben's safety. A telegram was dispatched to Tom, who was serving with the Royal Field Artillery.

The family attended Sunday Service at the Wesleyan Chapel in Edmondsley after a sleepless night. John Clayton, an inspiring Methodist local preacher, was elsewhere on Chester le Street Methodist circuit that morning. His thoughts must have been in Flanders. The children attended Sunday school as usual on the Sunday afternoon.

An attempt was made to carry on as normal in the hope that Ben had been captured, but a second telegram confirmed that Captain Clayton was not only missing but was known to have been badly wounded.

Chester le Street Chronicle, 7/9/1917 [with thanks to Derek Burgess]

The children were devastated as they waited for news. Priscilla, at 14, had already lost her elder sister when she was seven and Bill, only four when Daisy died, was only 11 when Ben was killed. Ellen Rita was nine. Isabel's children loved Ben as the kindly elder brother who acted as their go-between and confidant; throughout their lives they talked about him with pride and affection. News arrived that Captain Clayton had been awarded the Military Cross in Routine Orders of Major General Heneker on 22nd August 1917 for 'steadfast conduct in action'.

The grim consequences of Ben's death continued. His desolate father wrote querulous letters to the authorities. Major Jeffries, only briefly acquainted with Ben, wrote back, as did Major Ingham on his return to the shattered battalion.

John Clayton's sad queries established that in War Office parlance, Captain Clayton was indeed a 'Temporary Second Lieutenant, Acting Captain'.

Ben's trunk was dispatched to Edmondsley on 13th September 1917 and eventually arrived at Chester le Street station; it was delivered to School House on a dray by a North Eastern Railway carter. The last sketchbook was retrieved from it. Ben's clothes were removed, washed and sent to the Salvation Army; the trunk was carried up to the attic, and remained there until School House was sold in 1974.

Letters from the Military Secretary in Whitehall and from Major Ingham informed the Claytons that the body of a West Yorks Captain had been found on the 28th October 1917 in front of Zonnebeke Redoubt, newly captured by the Anzacs, and that the Burying Officer of the 1st ANZAC Corps had buried it in the flooded polder alongside many young Australians of 2nd Australian Division. It was impossible to identify the corpse further, but Ben Clayton was the only Captain in the West Yorkshire Regiment on the field that day, so Major Ingham decided to record Captain Clayton officially as 'Killed in Action'.

The state of the body was not mentioned but it seems likely that rats had eaten the viscera and that the hollow trunk may have been limbless and headless as a result of persistent bombardment by the British artillery over the ten weeks since Ben's death. This may account for the absence of the vulcanized asbestos identity tag. Captain Frank Hurley, Official Photographer to the Australian Imperial Force, comments on the bodies that were found every 20 paces or less around Zonnebeke Station: 'Some frightfully mutilated, without legs, arms and heads, and half covered in mud and slime.' (Abridged)

At the end of the Great War, known field graves were disinterred and concentrated in cemeteries by the War Graves Commission.

Some of the graves of the Anzac Forces killed in front of Zonnebeke were relocated to Hooge Crater Cemetery, close to the jumping off point of the 2nd West Yorks.

There is at least one grave of an unnamed soldier of the Prince of Wales's Own West Yorkshire Regiment amongst the 6,000 dead at Hooge Cemetery, so it is just possible that this is the final resting place of Captain Clayton.

Hooge Crater Cemetery, 2017

It seems more likely that Ben's body is under the plough in the field closest to Zonnebeke Redoubt, once again a Flanders Farmstead.

Zonnebeke Redoubt, 16/8/2017

His name is commemorated on Tyne Cot Memorial, originally a German stronghold near Zonnebeke, named, appropriately enough, by soldiers from the North East of England who detected a likeness between the flat-roofed German pillboxes and the single story workmens' cottages that were their homes back on the banks of the Tyne.

On Saturday 22nd March 1919, 19 months after Ben's death, the Committee of The Edmondsley Sailors and Soldiers Parcels Fund made presentations in Edmondsley School before a large crowd gathered to commemorate two local heroes, Captain B Clayton and

Private Joe Saltmarsh. Mr Hughes, the Secretary of the Committee, made the first presentation to Joe Saltmarsh, safely Home from the War. He pinned the Military Medal onto Private Saltmarsh's chest, awarded in Italy to Joe for walking alone through an enemy barrage to get help when his patrol was cut off in no man's land. Joe Saltmarsh was one of 110 young men who had gone to the Great War from Edmondsley, several of whom 'had left their bones in France'. The Secretary then handed Private Saltmarsh an inscribed gold watch. Amid cheers, Joe Saltmarsh thanked the Committee in suitable terms.

Mr Hughes then stated that it had been a pleasant duty to make a presentation to the person who had actually won it, but a different matter altogether to do so to the father of someone who had given his life for his country. Mr Hughes read out Captain Clayton's Military Cross citation from the London Gazette and asked John Clayton, the 'esteemed schoolmaster' if he would accept a gold watch 'which his son would have received had he lived'.

Mr Hughes then handed the watch, suitably inscribed, to Mr Clayton.

Front of gold fob watch

Back of gold watch with inscription

John Clayton replied graciously and said that he was very proud of Ben, to loud applause.

A programme of entertainment by Mr Sanderson's Greenbank (a neighbouring colliery village) Concert Party followed. This consisted of a clog dance, a humorous monologue, five solo songs and a duet, all accompanied by Mr Heslop on the piano. As soon as was seemly, a proud, but regretful and reflective John Clayton returned through the garden gate from the schoolyard to his quiet home in School House.

As Ben had no known grave, his father determined to go to Ypres to see where his son had died.

John Clayton leaving headmaster's study, 1922

He ordered the Michelin 'Guide to the Ypres Battlefield' from the Co-op in Chester le Street and, during school holidays in 1922, set off for Belgium. He had a working knowledge of French and German from his time at Durham University. He took the 10.45 p.m. sleeper from Durham Station to London. After breakfast next morning at the Great Northern Hotel, King's Cross, he took the Underground to Victoria and entrained for Dover. He must have reflected that his older boys had made the journey several times during the war, but in the end only one had come home. John Clayton crossed to Oostende on the Belgian Railway steam packet 'Ville de Liege' and from there went by train to Brugge (Bruges), where he booked into the Station Hotel. Next morning he set out for Ieper (Ypres).

He encountered a city still mainly in ruins, a desolate landscape, and numerous field cemeteries, some of which were being excavated

to allow re-siting of the dead. On the Menen (Menin) Road he was able
to look down at the devastation in the shallow valley of the Hanebeek.
The partly rebuilt ruins of Zonnebeke were visible about three miles
away on the opposite bank of the placid brook but he was unable to
learn more as there had been a series of battles to and fro around
Ypres after Ben's death. Unexploded ordnance was still a problem;
the combatants were either dead or had gone home. After prayer
and a period of reflection he decided that he would gain nothing by
remaining. Despondently he left on the day after he arrived.

His return ticket was not valid for a few days, so he revisited
Brugge, where he bought a print of the Dijver Canal,

Sketch of Dijver Canal, Brugge purchased by John Clayton in 1922

and then went on to Brussels and to Waterloo, where he bought
a brass tourist paperweight of the Waterloo Lion that stands on the
Memorial Mound. Both were displayed in School House until his
death in 1941.

John Clayton returned home a confused and disillusioned man.
The horrifying consequences of attritional warfare were unknown to
the British Public in the Great War. John's journey to Belgium led him
to a further struggle with his faith, but he decided not reject it. This

was to cause problems with his eldest surviving son, Tom, who had abandoned religion after his experiences at the front.

Ben Clayton had left a will dated 11/12/1915, drawn up by F Harle Esquire, a Solicitor of Chester le Street, that stated 'In the event of my death I give the whole of my property and effects to Isabella Clayton of School House Edmondsley', further confirmation of the loving relationship between Ben and his stepmother.

The Army Register of Soldiers' Effects records that Second Lieutenant B C Clayton had £106-10s-7d in his bank account when he was killed.

Army Register of soldiers' effects, 19/1/18

In October 1920 the War Office was still querying the Will, but a Letter of Administration from Mr Harle confirmed that Isabel Clayton was the sole beneficiary, and she eventually received all of Ben's money. On some calculations this could be the equivalent of about £16,300 today; an indication that Ben was not a profligate young officer while he was in France. John Clayton received an annual pension of £20 per annum, worth perhaps £3,000 per annum today.

For want of a better strategy, British Generals on the Western Front persisted for four years with an attritional conflict by day and a guerrilla in no man's land by night, where young men murdered each other with knives and clubs.

> *'Good morning, Good Morning' the General said,*
> *when we met him last week on our way to the Line*
> *Now the soldiers he smiled at are most of 'em dead*
> *and we're cursing his staff for incompetent swine.*

(Abridged) Siegfried Sassoon, 1918.

Ben Clayton's sketches give us an unusual insight into some of the methods the Infantry used to survive. Even in the quieter times he often portrays, the British Army suffered 35,000 casualties a month, a bloody end to the Victorian world of deference and religious faith. By Armistice Day about a third of those who had fought at the front were wounded or dead. Parents, relatives and girlfriends had encouraged their young men to enlist in 1914; they must accept some blame. The consequence of their thoughtless enthusiasm and the insouciant approach of many generals to the lives of their troops produced some 900,000 deaths in Great Britain and its Empire alone in just over 50 months of fighting.

The final Requiem for the Dead and for their parents must go to the last survivor of my family who could recall the Great War. Ben's youngest sister, Rita, was at her 80th Birthday Party in Cheltenham in 1988 when she was asked to describe her parents' reaction 71 years beforehand, on the day the telegram arrived to say that Ben was missing. She collected her thoughts for a moment, narrowed her eyes and replied quietly:

'Put it this way, there was never glad tiding in that house again'.

Ben's posthumous Military Cross

Ben's medals

Acknowledgements

This biography of the short life of my maternal uncle, Ben Clayton is inevitably an anthology. Ben was a 22-year-old artist and infantry officer when he was killed at the Battle of Passchendaele in 1917.

From the start of my research I have felt that I was standing on the shoulders of Giants. Captain Clayton's eighteen months on the Western Front can be followed a century later without difficulty because of the existence of three books: -

'With Bayonets Fixed' by John Sheen, published by Pen and Sword in 2013. This tells the story of the 12th Battalion of the Durham Light Infantry in the Great War. I have quoted verbatim from it.

'General Jack's Diary' by John Terraine, published by Cassell in 1964. This fascinating book records the exploits of the 2nd Battalion of the West Yorkshire Regiment. Ben Clayton is mentioned in it several times. I have frequently quoted from it.

'Twelve Days on the Somme' by Sidney Rogerson, published by Greenhill Books in 2006. This is a gripping record of wartime life in the 2nd Battalion of the West Yorkshire Regiment, albeit in a Company of the Battalion different from the one in which Ben served. Captain Rogerson and Second Lieutenant Clayton were exact contemporaries under the command of Lieutenant Colonel Jack for several months and shared many experiences in common. I have frequently quoted from Captain Rogerson's book. I note that he also was a talented artist. Without the existence of these books, and the dates in them, I could not have correlated the episodes depicted in Ben Clayton's dated 'Sketches from France' with the wartime experiences of the two battalions in which he served.

I have regularly consulted the Ph.D. thesis of Dr Alun Miles Thomas, published online in 2010 by the Centre for First World War Studies of the University of Birmingham. It is entitled 'British 8th Infantry Division on the Western Front 1914–1918'. I found it invaluable and have frequently quoted from it.

I have consulted the War Diaries of the 12th Battalion of the Durham Light Infantry and of the 2nd Battalion of The Prince of Wales's Own West Yorkshire Regiment and have quoted from them.

I have quoted from General Lord Rawlinson's 4th Army Records (Crown Copyright) about the 8th Division and about the Consequences of the Somme battle.

All the sketches and most of the photographs are from the archives of the Clayton Family, being either photographed by them or in their possession as postcards. The photographs of the Zonnebeke Battlefield were obtained from the Web.

A map of the Zonnebeke Battlefield was received from Simon Augustyn, a researcher at the Memorial Museum, Passchendaele. I am very grateful for his help.

I have read 'Goodbye to All That' by Robert Graves, first published in 1929 by Jonathan Cape and have quoted from it.

I have quoted from the poems of the 'War Poets'. Two are by Siegfried Sassoon M.C., and two are by Wilfred Owen M.C.

Finally, I could not have written this without the unstinting support of my wife, Marjorie, my children, Alistair, Richard and Victoria, and my two cousins Jill Parkes (nee Clayton), and John Russell Clayton Bowman. Together with me, Jill and John are the last of the Claytons of Edmondsley.

David Clayton Britton, 2017

Then out spake brave Horatius,
The Captain of the Gate:
"To every man upon this earth
Death cometh soon or late
And how can man die better
Than facing fearful odds,
For the ashes of his fathers,
And the temples of his gods."

The Lays of Ancient Rome, Horatius

Thomas Babington Macaulay, 1842

Leeds Training College War Memorial.
Ben's name is halfway down the third plaque from the left

INDEX